BON JOVI

Faith And Glory

THE OFFICIAL STORY
by Malcolm Dome

Published by: Castle Communications Plc
Book Division, A29 Barwell Business Park
Leatherhead Road, Chessington, Surrey KT9 2NY

Copyright © 1994 Castle Communications Plc

All pictures © 1994 Mark "Weiss Guy" Weiss printed by permission
exclusively for this official biography

Many thanks to Simon Kenton and all at Idols Licensing
for their extensive help in all matters pictorial.

Mark Weiss is represented by Idols Licensing

Design: Brian Burrows

ISBN 1-898141-30-4

BONJOVI

Faith and Glory

by Malcolm Dome

BON JOVI

Faith and Glory

CONTENTS

CHAPTER 1 • These Are The Days Of Our Lives 7

CHAPTER 2 • Life Before Bon Jovi 11

CHAPTER 3 • Into The Arena 23

CHAPTER 4 • Tough Talking Hombres 29

CHAPTER 5 • Volcanic Eruptions, Anyone? 35

CHAPTER 6 • Many A Slip . . . 45

CHAPTER 7 • The Consequence Of Fame 53

CHAPTER 8 • Let's Do The Monster Mash 63

CHAPTER 9 • Back On The Jersey Trail 75

CHAPTER 10 • Doc In The Dock 85

CHAPTER 11 • On The Skids 93

CHAPTER 12 • Going Solo 105

CHAPTER 13 • Richie Gets Strange 115

CHAPTER 14 • Oh, But Did You Hear What He Said . . . 121

CHAPTER 15 • Rediscovering The Faith 131

CHAPTER 16 • Into The Future 153

Faith and Glory

CHAPTER ONE

THESE ARE THE DAYS OF OUR LIVES

Visions and spirits. Words and emotions. Ten years. More, actually. From breathless hopes in New Jersey basements to motorcycle outriders in Madrid. Sometimes it was sunshine. Sometimes it was rain. Occasionally the storms broke. But then there came the heroics. The adulation. The satisfaction. The fulfilment. The release.

For me it's a whirl of jumbled memories, slightly burnt-out wires carrying my own personal history of Bon Jovi. First sight onstage at the vast Pacific Amphitheatre in Costa Mesa, California in April 1984. I won't forget that one in a hurry. The vast outdoor arena filled with Scorpions fans come to see the German band at the height of their commercial success. Who took notice of the raw, young support band? Personally, I didn't much go for their self-titled, debut album, even though it was becoming something of a cult classic among AOR aficionados.

Watching with indifference as the young Jon Bon Jovi led his troops through a professionally energetic set, I saw nothing to convince me that I was witnessing the birth pangs of a new species, that ten years on everybody would know who Bon Jovi are. Strange, but the microphone stand adorned with scarves merely had me snorting with derision. Somebody, I forget who, did confidently predict big things for this band at the end of that show. I think they worked for the record label - contractual optimism one might therefore call it.

Still, despite my misgivings at the time, that young band have gone on to achieve international fame and accolades. Perhaps, they have even performed beyond their wildest hopes and daring dreams, becoming a household name wherever rock music is part of the social fabric. This is their story. In particular, it is the story of Jon Bon Jovi, an unassuming lad from New Jersey who has the world at his feet. In parts it is the story of triumph through willpower and struggle. In others, it is the story of talent for once coming to the surface and gaining orbital velocity. And in a musical world where today's hero is tomorrow's tattered headline, Bon Jovi have been a consistent beacon. Praise indeed.

Anyway, before entering the portals of the book in all its glory, let me take this opportunity to thank a few people - or a lot of people. Ready? Here goes:

Thanks are due to Phil Scott, Laurie Pryor, Sonia Bailey, Iain Davie, Nicola O'Donegan and all at Castle Communications Plc and Penguin Books, Margaret Sterlacci, Paul Korzilius and everybody at BJM, Sylvie Simmons, Arlett 'Queenie' Vereecke, Phil Alexander, Dave Ling, Lynn and Mark Putterford, Steve ''old Up' McTaggart, Xavier Russell, Ray Palmer, Pete Cronin, Jerry Ewing, Kirk Blows, Mark Blake,

Paul Henderson, Denise Stillie, Annick Barbaria, Shaun Hutson (got you back, mate), Krusher Joule, Geezer Joseph, Colin Burns, Sue Hyams, Nick White, Jackie The Cat, Sharon Black, Fiona Flanagan, Liz Wells, Sophie Williams, Gem Howard, Gillian Porter, Billy Arnold and Chris Roberts.

Thanks for inspiration to: Everton FC (for the hours of frustration and occasional moments of fulfilment), my family, The St. Moritz Club (free drink, guys?), numerous alcoholic beverages, the Monte Bello restaurant (free meal, guys?), plus too many great sounds, TV shows and films to mention.

And, of course, everlasting thanks to the Bon Jovi fellas (Jon, Richie, David, Tico and Alec) for all the good times and the amazing music. Without them this would not have been possible.
This book is dedicated to those with the vision to dream and the spirit to believe.

CHAPTER TWO

LIFE BEFORE BON JOVI

*L*ook, before I get stuck into the body of this book there are a couple of things that must be made clear. Firstly, this isn't an exposé, a let's-tell-the-world-about-the-scandal-in Bon Jovi affair. If you're expecting something of that order, then you've got the wrong book. Moreover, you won't find enormous insight into Jon Bon Jovi's personal life. He didn't want it that way - and he's quite right. Perhaps one day, Jon - who is inevitably the central figure in all of this verbiage - will sit down and write his autobiography, whilst bouncing his grandchildren on his knee. If he does, then that would be the appropriate time for the story of Jon Bon Jovi from the inside.

No, the criteria for 'Faith And Glory' is to tell the story of Jon's professional life. Simple as that.

Secondly, this is not a sycophantic aren't-they-wonderful-in-all-they-do kind of affair. Those sort of books serve no purpose whatsoever - least of all in painting an accurate picture of the band. I know of one author who wrote the official biography of a band and was told, he couldn't even mention a particular controversial incident in their career - despite the fact that it was well documented.

This did not happen with Bon Jovi. Everything essential is here. And I haven't held back from criticising the band, if I genuinely felt it to be necessary.

Finally, I want to point out that if you're looking for a fact-by-fact report on the band's history...Well, forget it. Those sort of books are inevitably boring. I'll leave it to a trained statistician to write the Bon Jovi factfile. Me? I'm more interested in trying to get to the heart of the band, what makes them tick. Thus I haven't mentioned every single gig Bon Jovi ever did, nor have I tried to recall every damn song they've written. I wanted this book to be an entertaining read, with freshly laundered anecdotes peppering the pages. I hope once you've finished reading this, you'll feel I've succeeded. If not, blame me - the buck stops here! Right, now all that is out of the way, I'm gonna start off by breaking one of the rules I set out above. Because in order to understand and appreciate the story of Bon Jovi in its proper perspective, you have to have at least some understanding of Jon Bon Jovi's early days. So...

Jon was born on March 2, 1962 in Perth Amboy, New Jersey, about 25 miles north of Astbury Park, made famous by Bruce Springsteen, one of Jon's real heroes. He was the oldest of three brothers (the others being Anthony and Matt), born to Carol and John Bongiovi Snr. Carol had been crowned Miss Erie, Pennsylvania in her younger days and went on to work briefly as a Playboy Bunny. And perhaps it was this background that enabled Carol in particular to encourage Jon when he showed aspirations himself of moving into the entertainment world. It wasn't a case of trying to live vicariously through her son, more an understanding of his dream, and an appreciation of her own frustration at not making it happen for herself. Jon's parents certainly never pushed him into becoming a musician, but once he'd made up his mind, their support became crucial and vital. However, reports that John Snr. had ambitions in his early years of becoming a singer are erroneous.

Unlike many, Jon has a valued and close relationship with his family to this day. His mother, in fact, helps to run the Bon Jovi fan club and is clearly intensely proud of her son's achievements.

When Jon was four, the family moved to a house in Sayreville, New Jersey - and that house was to become famous during the 'Slippery When Wet' period of the band when it was bought by MTV, who then promptly gave it away in one of their more audacious competitions.

When he was seven years old, Jon got his first guitar, bought for him by his mother. But in typical infant style, the future rock star showed no inclination towards strumming the instrument. Unlike Mozart, Jon was certainly not going to write a great piece music before his tenth birthday! But, eventually Jon began to take lessons from a local music teacher, Al Parinello. "I wanted to learn guitar at the time so that I could pick up girls!" admits Jon, but he quickly showed a musical application, which was eventually to lead him into forming his very first band, Raze. Originally called Starz, the name change was forced on the young Jon Bongiovi and his fledgling cohorts because of the existence already of a comparatively successful American band under that banner. But the band didn't exactly set the world, or even New Jersey, alight.

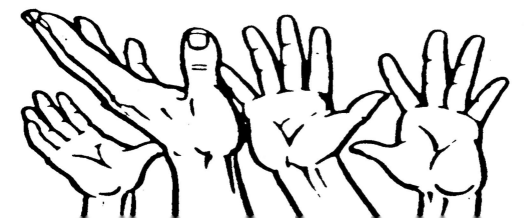

BON JOVI

15

Raze played their first ever gig at a talent contest held at Sayreville High School, where Jon was ensconced as a pupil. They performed three songs on that fateful night, namely 'Strutter' by Kiss, 'Johnny B. Goode' (yep, that old standard) and 'Taking Care Of Business' from Bachman-Turner Overdrive. But any hopes they might have had of setting out on the yellow brick road to fame and fortune were dashed. "Er, we came in last," laughs Jon at the memory of his first foray into the heady world of rock'n'roll. But the spark had been ignited and wasn't going to be put out very easily.

Whilst at Sayreville High School, Jon attempted to expand his repertoire by appearing in a version of the hit stage musical 'Mame' - he got the minor part of Junior Babcock. Years later, Jon was to get a minor walk-on part in a film, 'Young Guns II', for which movie he wrote the music. Jon's role was one of those blink-and-you'll-miss-him affairs. But he has never harboured aspirations to be an actor - offers have been made over the years, but nothing he has considered worthwhile.

Meantime, back in the late '70s at Sayreville High, Jon was plotting a more serious successor to Raze. With classmate Willy Hercek, he put together a band called The Atlantic City Expressway (also known simply as ACE - much easier to digest). This was basically an R&B ten-piece which began life just playing at local parties. However, it was to provide Jon with his first taste of genuine gigs in clubs and bars around New Jersey. Among the musicians involved in this alliance was a certain keyboardsman called David Rashbaum, who of course was to play a major role in the development of Bon Jovi, under the name David Bryan.

Born on February 7, 1962 in Edison, New Jersey, David had been trained as a classical pianist since the age of seven. He had played in a couple of local bands prior to ACE, including covers band Transition, but nothing that had made any impact. However, he soon struck up a strong friendship with Jon.

The Atlantic City Expressway quickly built up a good local following, playing anywhere and everywhere. Jon himself once quaintly summed up his determination to get the band into every conceivable venue thus: "I'd have played a pay toilet and used my own change!" And it was at this time that Jon began to augment the usual staple of covers with some of his own material. More importantly, the band were getting noticed. Celebrities, including Springsteen, would regularly come down to the gigs and jam with the young musicians. Things were on the move. However, ACE were not destined to last much longer.

Rashbaum left to enrol in the world-renowned Juilliard School Of Music in New York City, in order to pursue more seriously his classical training. And Jon followed suit in quitting ACE (who quickly split up), hoping to find a way of taking his aspirations to the next level. Eventually, he was to join up with The Rest, who played new wave music, something of a departure for Jon. The band was built around the talents of musician/ songwriter Jack Ponti, a man who in subsequent years made his name behind the scenes by writing and producing. Ponti never quite had what it took to make it on his own, but he soon recognised that Jon had something truly special. And the experience The Rest gave Jon was invaluable. Both Billy Squier and Southside Johnny - the former beginning to make an impact as a major rock artiste, the latter one of New Jersey's legendary R&B performers and another hero of Jon's - produced demos for the band. They even got so far as to interest both Capitol and Columbia Records, but in neither case was the interest sufficient to lead anywhere.

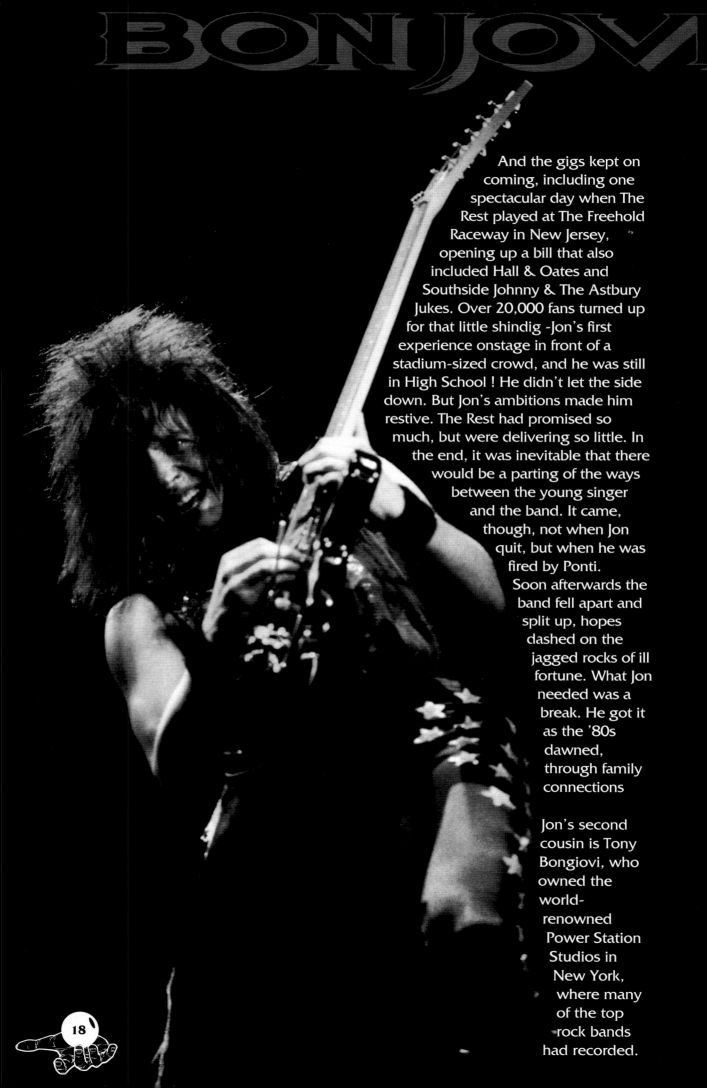

BON JOVI

And the gigs kept on coming, including one spectacular day when The Rest played at The Freehold Raceway in New Jersey, opening up a bill that also included Hall & Oates and Southside Johnny & The Astbury Jukes. Over 20,000 fans turned up for that little shindig -Jon's first experience onstage in front of a stadium-sized crowd, and he was still in High School ! He didn't let the side down. But Jon's ambitions made him restive. The Rest had promised so much, but were delivering so little. In the end, it was inevitable that there would be a parting of the ways between the young singer and the band. It came, though, not when Jon quit, but when he was fired by Ponti.

Soon afterwards the band fell apart and split up, hopes dashed on the jagged rocks of ill fortune. What Jon needed was a break. He got it as the '80s dawned, through family connections

Jon's second cousin is Tony Bongiovi, who owned the world-renowned Power Station Studios in New York, where many of the top rock bands had recorded.

Bongiovi himself was also a high class producer and engineer. Tony took him on as what was termed an 'artist in development'. He had seen The Rest in action in 1980 when there was label interest in the band, and according to his own account liked what he saw of Jon. The latter, though, has always insisted that Tony hated the band. There you go, you pays your money and you takes your pick.

Whatever, after the demise of The Rest, Jon began life at The Power Station in September. He wasn't exactly set to work at the executive level. Being an 'artist in development', getting $50 per week, meant that he also had to undertake a number of menial tasks into the bargain, all of which he tackled with a zest born out of his inner belief and confidence that, at last, there was hope on the horizon.

"I was the errand boy, the person who swept the studio, made the coffee...For two years I slept on the floor at the studio and learnt all about the music business."

But whilst he was doing all of this, Jon also got the chance to meet many of the top musicians working at The Power Station, and to pick up tricks of the trade. He was initially paid the princely sum of $52.50 per week for his efforts, eventually rising to $125 by the time his stint was over. But he got invaluable exposure to the mechanics of recording, through soaking up the vibes emanating from the likes of the Rolling Stones and Aerosmith. Jon also got the chance to record demos during 'down time' at the studio, those hours (usually very early morning or very late at night) when no-one else was using the studio. In this manner, he cut hour-upon-hour of tape. At this point, Jon had no band to work with, so he either grabbed hold of whoever was around to help him cut the demos, or else played on his own - dedication, though, was always his watchword.

Eventually, though, Jon did put together a line-up for recording purposes under the name of The Lechers, who played small bars and even worked on original material. However, this wasn't exactly a permanent band, with constant line-up changes being forced on Jon, dependent on who was actually available at any one time. But the next band he put together was to have far-reaching ramifications.

It was called The Wild Ones, and was to provide the basis for Bon Jovi. It was at this point that Jon wrote a song called 'Runaway', which seemed to have the potential to become something of a hit single. Tony Bongiovi, recognising that at last his investment was beginning to pay off, got together a recording line-up to lay down the number at The Power Station and the demo was sent to every record company on the east coast of America. The tape was sent out under the name of 'Johnny B.', and also included three other original tracks. But there were still frustrating times ahead for Jon, by now inured to the unpredictability of rock'n'roll. A showcase was set up at The Ritz in New York for The Wild Ones, but this went horribly wrong. Opening for Southside Johnny, Jon had to use a stand-in rhythm section, which proved disastrous.

But Jon wasn't about to give in. Taking time out only to perform the lead vocal on a track titled 'R2D2 - I Wish You A Merry Christmas' for a festive cash-in album called 'Star Wars Christmas Album' (produced by Tony Bongiovi), the singer gathered together his determination, and accompanied by David headed for Los Angeles and set up base camp at the A-1 Motel. They then proceeded to hit every record label in town, hoping that somebody would get hooked on The Wild Ones - nobody did. Dead ends were piling faster than empty bottles at a pill poppers' convention. But a stroke of good fortune - the one break Jon had been angling for - was about to take place in New York.

Jon's tape of the song 'Runaway' was entered for a local radio station talent contest going under the name of 'Rock To Riches'. It was being organised by new classic rock radio station WAPP on Long Island (sadly no longer in existence) and the idea of presenting Jon's tape came from a former employee at The Power Station, Ray Willhard (an assistant engineer and aspiring manager). It was he who took down the tape to the station, with Jon, where it was promptly accepted for the contest. "Being a new station, I thought that they might be more receptive to my tape" explains Jon of this decision . The power and quality of the tape ensured that Jon comfortably won his regional heat in this contest, as a result of which 'Runaway' appeared on a compilation album put together by WAPP of unsigned acts. Commercially available in the New York area, the idea behind this album was also to provide stations owned by WAPP's parent company, the mighty Doubleday, with tracks for airplay. Also featured on this record were Twisted Sister and Zebra, both of whom were to get record deals. Suddenly, Jon's original version of 'Runaway' was getting national airplay exposure - and if you're lucky enough to possess a copy of this record, aside from giving it to me, I would hang on to it for dear life - it's worth a few pennies!

By now, there was a genuine buzz building up for Jon, almost by accident. The best-laid plans of various aficionados in an attempt to break him hadn't worked, but fate was taking a strong hand in matters. And, as is the norm with the music industry, the very record companies who had not so long before turned their backs on Jon, now began courting him. He was a hot item on the agenda at almost every A&R meeting in New York - the race was on. It was time for that great game of 'Let's Make A Deal'.

CHAPTER THREE

INTO THE ARENA

Two labels quickly emerged as the frontrunners to sign Jon Bon Jovi (by now Jon was operating under his own name, with a loose alliance of musicians - the name 'Wild Ones' was quickly dropped). They were Atlantic Records and PolyGram Records. Both could offer the band clout, in terms of financial support and artistic endeavour. Jon decided to put to good use the practises he had picked up whilst working at The Power Station by cleverly playing one off against the other. It was a case of seeing just how far he could raise the ante. In the end, though, PolyGram won the race for his prized signature.

The man responsible for getting Jon to PolyGram was Englishman Derek Shulman. A musician in his own right, Shulman had played with such bands as Gentle Giant (cult status only) and established a good reputation for knowing what he was talking about when it came to spotting musical talent. Employed in the A&R department at PolyGram in New York, Shulman had every confidence that Jon and Co. would break big, thereby making his own position secure. The lot of A&R people is always fraught with the fear of failure. But one success can virtually set you up for life. Shulman achieved this with Bon Jovi (as the band were to become later on), and then followed that up by taking Jon's advice by snapping up Cinderella - and watching them go through the roof. He then inked a contract with controversial sub-Zeppelin band Kingdom Come, before moving on to become President of Atco Records, home of the likes of AC/DC and Yes. These days, he runs his own label, Collision Records.

Back in 1983, Shulman landed his fish on July 1, the day Jon inked a deal with PolyGram, and then celebrated by investing in a sports car, as well as treating his perennially supportive parents to a deserved holiday. Jon had elected to withdraw from the 'Rock To Riches' final just prior to signing his recording deal, having gained what he wanted. Let somebody else earn the kudos of winning. He had other things to plan. The first step was to put together a permanent working band, something he hadn't been privy to for a while, not since The Wild Ones lost their rhythm section.

David Rashbaum was, by this time, very much in the harness. But who else could he get? First up was bassist Alec John Such. Born on November 14 1952 (although he shed several years in the 'official' Bon Jovi biography put together by PolyGram, in order to make him seem closer in age to Jon), Alec had made a living by combining session work with a number of top touring artistes with a position in local New Jersey covers bands.

And Alec in turn brought in drummer Hector 'Tico' Torres. Born on October 7 1953, Tico was without a doubt an in-demand drummer. he had played on numerous albums through the years and was a hardened studio veteran. At the time of the offer from Jon, Tico had been working out with an American band called Franke And The Knockouts, signed to RCA. They had released several albums which caused a minor ripple in AOR circles, but no more. Perhaps the most interesting thing about Franke And The Knockouts was the fact that they were managed by one Burt Ward - you might recall him in tights and cape paying the role of 'Robin The Boy Wonder' in the camp and cult '60s TV series 'Batman'! Oh, and Franke was Frankie Previtt who was to win an oscar for the music in the movie 'Dirty Dancing'.

Anyway, when Jon approached Tico to join with his growing band of merry men, the drummer readily agreed to throw in his lot with this young band of hopefuls. Needing a guitarist to complete the line-up, Jon turned at first to his old school pal Dave 'Snake' Sabo. Thus the Jon Bon Jovi group had a form of shape. They were rarin' to go, and Jon was preparing to take on the world.

However, this was not meant to develop into a full blown band, but rather a bunch of musos temporarily backing Jon, whilst he developed his musical muscle. But fate was to take a hand, enter one Richard Stephen Sambora. Born in Woodbridge, New Jersey on July 11, 1959, Richie, like Jon, came from something of an entertainment background. His parents were both ballroom dancers. Richie pretty much taught himself to play the guitar from an early age, although like so many kids he did have piano lessons (as well as accordion and trumpet). He put his talent to good use at first with a band called Mercy, signed to Led Zeppelin's Swan Song label.

"Mercy were something of a progressive band," recalls Richie. The irony of being on the same label as Zeppelin is that Sambora himself was, and remains, a massive fan of Jimmy Page, just one of the guitarist whose influence one can hear in his playing.

"Richie still remains in awe of Jimmy," laughs Jon. "In fact, on a recent tour of Europe, Jimmy came to see us in Amsterdam. He turned up backstage after the show, but I had to try and keep him out of the dressing room, because Richie was in there naked! Imagine how embarrassed he would have been to have Jimmy walk in and see him naked."

As with Jon, Richie has always remained a steadfast fan of music and his original heroes. Age and success hasn't blunted his touchingly naive faith in the power and emotion of music. After Mercy, Richie joined up with a funk band called Duke Williams And The Extremes, who were signed to Capricorn Records. but their style didn't really fit in with his aspirations or technique. Richie also tried his hand at acting, when he got a small role (playing the part of a musician) in the film 'Staying Alive'. In this respect, he at least had outdone Jon at this stage in their careers; the latter had auditioned for the lead role in the musical 'Footloose' - he failed to get the role, not surprising considering that the part required somebody with dancing abilities. Jon has never claimed any great talents in this direction.

Back in '83, Alec and Tico persuaded Richie to come down and see Jon Bon Jovi perform. The guitarist had just finished a stint on the road supporting Joe Cocker in a band called The Message, and was planning on doing some studio recording when he got the call. Richie was staying in Chicago, so when Jon Bon Jovi came to town Sambora, ambled down to take a look. He was impressed. Walking backstage, Richie met Jon, greeting him with the simple statement that he was the guitarist Jon should be working with! A propitious moment. Bold and arrogant as this claim might have been, it was to prove correct. Jon realised that 'Snake' wasn't quite right for the band, and hired Richie. 'Snake' himself went on to form Skid Row and find success in his own right - the pai were also to cross paths again on a professional level later in their respective careers. Suddenly, Jon had a real band around him of top class musicians.

With everything in place, it was decided to drop the name Jon Bon Jovi. It felt wrong. But what could replace it? Victory was jokingly suggested and dropped. Johnny Lightning was another possibility. But nothing felt right. In the end, it would be Polygram head of A&R Jerry Jaffe who came up with the idea of just using the name Bon Jovi. What made it even more appropriate was the fact that Jon was the only member of the band actually signed to PolyGram. All the others were effectively hired hands.

Faith And Glory

The band warmed up their chops by going out on tour to build a momentum and work out the hitches. It was dubbed 'The Stationwagon Tour' and saw them play everywhere and in all manner of venues - from clubs to arenas. they even got to play at Madison Square Garden opening up for ZZ Top wherein they were scouted by several top managers. It was valuable experience that was to prove crucial in honing the band's skills.

Jon eventually signed a management deal with McGhee Entertainment in New York, who also looked after Mötley Crüe. It was a fledgling organisation, but Doc McGhee and his partner Doug Thaler had vast experience in the music industry and were confident they could give the band the necessary back-up.

Recalling those long gone days, Jon has little sentiment.

"When I look back there's nothing I miss from those early days apart from the innocence and fun. It was really hard work."

The next stage, however, was to take the Bon Jovi sound onto the world stage. And the first move in this endeavour necessitated the recording of the band's debut album.

CHAPTER FOUR

TOUGH TALKING HOMBRES

Perhaps it was inevitable that Bon Jovi would work with Tony Bongiovi on their debut album. But he wasn't alone in handling the production chores. The veteran Lance Quinn (Bongiovi's partner) helped out in the studio, inevitably The Power Station. The result was the 'Bon Jovi' album. Originally, this was to be released under the title of 'Tough Talk' - can you imagine if the band had kept the monicker of The Wild Ones and released an album called 'Tough Talk'? It would have immediately tagged them as second-raters! Fortunately, good sense prevailed and the Bon Jovi tag appeared as both band and album title.

The cover of the record boasted a shot of Jon crossing a lamp-lit New York street staring into camera. In the middle of the road stands a sultry femme fatale. From the start, Bon Jovi wasn't just the name of the band, it signified where PolyGram at least felt the fivesome's fortune lay - in Jon himself.

Personally, I have never been overly fond of the 'Bon Jovi' album. Raved about in melodic hard rock circles on its US release in January 1984 (a European release followed suit three months later - it was the only time that a Bon Jovi album wasn't granted simultaneous worldwide release), to me the record always sounded rather stilted and slightly dated. However, there was no doubting the power and performance on certain cuts. The revamped version of 'Runaway' (which was to provide the band with their first US Top 40 single, when it peaked at Number 39) has charm and a certain elegance, whilst 'Breakout' is a tough, stylised passion-play. 'Get Ready' is rather a parabolic anthem, and 'Shot Through The Heart' is an insistent, copiously glorious pop-rocker. But the rest of the album remains eminently mediocre - at least in my estimation, anyway. But the album garnered very positive reviews on both sides of the Atlantic.

In the UK, Paul Suter of Kerrang! claimed:

"Jon Bon Jovi has assembled a band of classic finesse and brutal strength...The material is dramatic and energetic, and blessed with a commerciality that should ensure plentiful sales."

The record also featured a guest performance from big time Canadian star Aldo Nova. The Montreal-based man had broken through into the big time with his first album a couple of years previously, and now he was brought in to add his own talents to those of the assembled Jovis. Years later, Jon was to repay Aldo for his help by signing him to his own label when Nova couldn't get arrested anywhere else.

"This was the best album we could have made at the time," recalls Jon. "I have to say that it was exciting making the album and I am proud of certain parts. 'Runaway' and 'Shot Through The Heart' stand out as still being worthy."

One thing that Bon Jovi did on the album they were not to repeat was to record someone else's song, namely Mark Avsec's 'She Don't Know Me', one of the true low spots in the band's career. The only other time the Jovis took to doing a cover was for charity reasons, when they recorded a version of Thin Lizzy's 'The Boys Are Back In Town' for an anti-drugs campaign, helmed by manager Doc McGhee - we'll get to that shortly.

The album reached Number 43 in the US and even entered the UK charts, making it up to the dizzy heights of Number 71 in the national charts. But whilst this might seem chicken feed in the wake of what was to occur just two years later, nonetheless it was a beginning.

Bon Jovi also swept themselves into the burgeoning video market by cutting promotional footage for 'Runaway'. The result was dreadful and something the band recall with a hideous shudder.

"The video for 'Runaway' was the biggest piece of shit I'd ever seen. The producer for the video didn't even attempt to follow the song's storyline, instead he had this idea of using his niece in a concept piece that made no sense. And the band, all of us just came out of it looking like complete assholes."

The video was shot over a period of three days, down in a disused warehouse. "I recall how excited we all were when we drove into Manhattan to our manager's office to watch it. Anyway, after the screening, we just sat there in complete silence - the song had been ruined. I felt like giving it all up and going back to work in the shoe shop where I was once employed (Kinney Shoes, where he was employed at the age of 16). The video cost the band $60,000 to shoot. As Jon told Phil Alexander at RAW: "I learnt a new word that day. The record company lawyer walked right in after we'd watched the video and said, 'Isn't it sooo wonderful?' And we went, 'Yeah!' And he said, 'Yeah, and it's recoupable too!' And I said, 'Great! It's recoupable.' I went outside and said, 'What the f**k does that mean?!' We learnt from our mistakes."

The disaster over the video notwithstanding, the band were making rapid progress in their stride towards establishing themselves as a premier rock outfit for the '80s. In America, they jumped on tour with various acts, including the Scorpions, the exposure doing much to augment what had already been achieved via the album. As I said in Chapter One, I caught the Bon Jovi show for the first time in Costa Mesa, California, when they supported the Scorps. I was not wholly impressed - and said so in a review from the gig published in Kerrang!. That review precipitated a shoal of letters supporting the band, and led me to admit that there was an undoubted momentum carrying them forward towards their prescribed goal.

In Britain, the band chose to tour for the first time supporting a rock legend - Kiss, also signed to the PolyGram stable. The shows kicked off September 30 in Brighton, traversing the country throughout the next two weeks, taking in dates at Southampton, Cornwall, Manchester, Glasgow, Edinburgh, Newcastle, Leicester, Ipswich, Stafford, Leeds and London. The climax of the tour occurred at the Wembley Arena over two nights during mid-October -a momentous occasion for the still-inexperienced Bon Jovi boys. And there was little doubt that by the time the band hit the UK, they were considerably improved as compared to what I had seen in the States.

Talking just prior to the Kiss tour, Jon had emphasised to Sylvie Simmons of Kerrang! just how much he thought they'd improved as a unit.

"With the Scorpions we got no soundchecks, minimal stage room and use of the PA rig and the lighting. There were a lot of things working against us. I personally tried to do the best that I could.

"But I never try to satisfy the critics. I just want to satisfy the kids and myself. What I do onstage is me - I can't pretend to be anything else. Some might think it's calculated, but I think it's Bon Jovi. We all put 100 per cent effort in to what we do every night. We are truly a family."

Certainly, the fans lapped up the Bon Jovi 45-minute onslaught. They chose the material carefully from their debut album, and built a sensible, hard-hitting set. Britain was indeed to play an important part in the establishment of the band. Being a smaller country, it is perhaps a little easier to make an impact, and once the foundations had been laid, Bon Jovi were quick to seize their opportunity. With the news of their success in Britain having spread back to America, it reaffirmed their growing reputation. The march was on.

BON JOVI

Faith And Glory

CHAPTER FIVE

VOLCANIC ERUPTIONS, ANYONE?

Like most bands whose debut album does reasonably well, there was immediate pressure on Bon Jovi to go back into the studio and record a second album. Thus, came '7800 Degrees Fahrenheit'. For this task, the band chose to part company with Tony Bongiovi. the circumstances are still shrouded in something of a mystery. Jon and Tony haven't spoken since. The latter felt that all the hard work and effort he had put into developing Jon's latent talents (not to mention the money that had been expended) deserved something of a financial reward. However, it seems that he chose to try and exercise this demand by getting Jon to sign a publishing deal with him at the time 'Runaway' was first written, wherein Tony would make money through royalties on any songs Jon subsequently wrote. The naive Jon, only 20 at the time, readily agreed to sign this contract, but quickly regretted it.

Thus, Jon chose at the appropriate moment to sever any connections with Tony Bongiovi and The Power Station. He was going to stand on his own two feet and wasn't to be intimidated by previous, ill-conceived agreements. With Tony Bongiovi out of the picture, Jon turned to Lance Quinn (who had dissolved his partnership with Bongiovi in 1984) for the production of the new album. Operations were also moved from New York to The Warehouse Studios in Philadelphia. They shacked up in a small apartment and got down to the business of working on the new album. However, there were distractions in the lives of certain of the band personnel. Both Tico and Alec were going through divorces at the time, and the whole atmosphere was rather depressed within the camp.

"Strangely enough all the problems that we were encountering at the time made us stronger as a unit. We were really beginning to bond. Tico and Alec were having their domestic difficulties, and I had just broken up with my girlfriend, which meant that I felt awful. So, some of the songs on the album are pretty sad and miserable. It just reflected the way I was feeling at the time. That's all you can expect from any record - a reflection of the time it was made."

There is certainly a darkness of thought and application on '7800...', which took its title enigmatically from the temperature inside a volcano at the time of eruption. But this is the very thing that made me prick up my ears and realise that the band had made giant strides forward. To this day, '7800...' is the record regarded by most people as the band's one flop - because it didn't break through the million-selling barrier in the US. but upon examination of the music prowess and content, there is no question '7800...' was a precise precursor for what was to follow. It had real emotion and maturity. Its darker side, as evinced on such tracks as 'The Hardest Part Is The Night' (wherein Jon displayed openly for the first time a rich talent for penning meaningful, articulate lyrics), 'Price Of Love' and 'Only Lonely', made me at least understand and appreciate that here was a band with far more to offer than just pretty faces and pleasant tunes. I became a Bon Jovi fan the moment I heard the record. Which is wierd, because most Bon Jovi fans would agree that this was the band's worst album! Strange but true.

For those wishing more uptempo fare, there was always the likes of 'In And Out Of Love', a precision-planted shadow bomber of road warrior viability, and 'King Of The Mountain'. In the meantime, 'Silent Night' proved to be a delicate ballad that eschewed any pretence towards deliberate heart-string tugging, and 'Tokyo Road' drew on the band's experiences on their first tour of Japan during the promotion of the 'Bon Jovi' record. The band had been an immediate hit there.

The release of '7800 Degrees Fahrenheit' in April 1985 was greeted with a mixed response. PolyGram had hoped that this would propel the band into the stratosphere. It didn't happen. The album limped up the charts in the America, stuttering at the gold standard, selling just in excess of half-a-million copies. It was a bitter disappointment for many. All the hopes and aspirations evinced by the 'Bon Jovi' album had been virtually put on hold.

The band went out on the road in the US supporting Los Angeles rockers Ratt. How ironic. The latter had achieved huge sales (multi-platinum - over three million) with their first full album in 1984, 'Out Of The Cellar', but that was to be the peak of their success. By the time 'Invasion Of Your Privacy' was issued as the follow-up in '85 and Ratt set out for the first time to headline arenas, they were unknowingly in decline. Bon Jovi, on the hand, had only temporarily stalled.

And the crowd reaction on that tour actually suggested the support act were getting a better response than the headliners. '7800...' might have failed to ignite the charts, and set the cash registers clicking like inebriated locusts, but the band were more popular than ever. It was as if the audience was telling the Jovis that one failed record was certainly not going to deprive them of their rightful, and eventual position of pre-eminence. Bon Jovi, feeling this strong vein of belief, reacted accordingly. And Ratt, fearful of being eclipsed by their opening band, started to impose restrictions on BJ, such as the absence of soundchecks and the limitations of stage space.

All this did was to irritate Bon Jovi and further sharpen their resolve. Relations with Ratt deteriorated, especially between Jon and the headliners egocentric vocalist Stephen Pearcy, but that was channelled into a furious spasm of energy by the New Jersey lads on every night of the tour - frustrations transformed into aggression onstage.

It's amusing to note that in subsequent years, Ratt slid further into obscurity as Bon Jovi headed ever upwards. And in 1993, Pearcy's new band Arcade (Ratt having split up) supported Bon Jovi on selected US dates.

"It was strange and funny having Stephen's band open for us," recalls Jon. "But I felt in no way a sense of triumph. It was just the way things go. Trouble is Stephen still can't work an audience that well!"

But, whilst '7800 Degrees Fahrenheit' had fallen foul to the supposed and infamous 'Second Album Syndrome' (the maxim that somehow most bands' second record falls down because of a combination of time pressure and expectation - I still maintain that '7800...' is a glorious exception to that rule, but maybe I am a lonely figure in this respect), nonetheless there were certainly some dramatic strides made by the band during the subsequent tour.

In the US, Bon Jovi were invited to participate in the high profile charity show Farm Aid. Conceived by John Cougar Mellencamp and Willie Nelson, this was almost a riposte to the furore and hype surrounding Live Aid, in that it set out to raise funds for people in need on America's doorstep - specifically, farmers in the American mid-west region, who were suffering cruel deprivations under the siege of Reagan economics. Bon Jovi appeared at an ungodly hour of the morning for just eight minutes in total, but it was front of some 83,000 fans on the site in Montana, as well as millions more on TV. This exposure for the band was a vital breakthrough, and the performance included one surprising entry, namely a new song titled 'Heart Of America'. It was written virtually on the spot, but sowed the seeds for the positive attitude and message than Bon Jovi have made very much part of their psyche. There is no doubt that Bon Jovi have taken a very assertive role in reflecting and tapping into the huge panorama of positivism that also pervades America - especially in mid-west. They are masters at capturing the essence of belief and faith in the human spirit. 'Heart Of America' offered the message of 'we can do things if we all pull together'.

In many ways, Jon Bon Jovi has taken the same path as John Cougar Mellencamp, starting out as something of a pretty boy, shallow-hearted rocker (at least in public consumption), but finally being given the opportunity to be taken serious as a caring musician. At the time of '7800...', he was still some way short of getting the respect he was striving towards. But there was no doubting his commitment to the cause and his genuine interest in music at all levels.

I found this out when I first met Jon. It was in August 1985, a few days prior to the band appearing at the Castle Donington Monsters Of Rock Festival in the heart of England. We had conversed previously, Jon had even taken to sending me postcards from various parts of the world during the tour to promote the debut album - simple, little, pleasant messages in the wake of my negative review of that Costa Mesa show. He felt that I had been unfair to him and set out to try and change my mind, not through strong-arm tactics, but simply through the agency of gaining my attention. Eventually, when I saw the band supporting Ratt early in 1985 at the outset of the '7800...' tour at the Meadowlands Arena in New Jersey, he finally got his way - I was totally hooked and thoroughly impressed with what was on offer. I was therefore intrigued as to how the two of us would get on. But he quickly set me at ease and greatly impressed me with his timing and touch as an interviewee. My commission was to get Jon to review a batch singles for Kerrang!. We didn't have long, but he sat and listened intently to every last note of every single track. And his comments were objective, helpful and full of constructive criticism.

Jon seemed determined to give every band a chance, however awful the music seemed on first listen. He knew only too well how difficult it was to get to the stage of recording anything for public consumption. His own recording career was only 18 months old.

And he threw this attitude into his comments. I doubt very much whether anybody else would have taken so much trouble over such an arduous task - he was a shining example also to journalists who regularly tackle the job. And what a contrast he made to another musician playing on the Donington bill, who was also brought in to review the singles. I shan't name the other chap, but he could scarcely be bothered to hear any record beyond the first 30 seconds, and his comments showed little enthusiasm.

Bon Jovi were invited to appear on the bill at Donington after a hugely successful debut headlining trek around the UK in May of 1985. They selected five venues in Manchester, Birmingham, London, Newcastle and Edinburgh and sold them out, with Canadian chanteuse Lee Aaron in support. It was a tour that took the band to a new level in Britain - and also spread the word back to America that the band were ready to move into a headlining status back there as well.

Everyone who was there will certainly recall the band's appearance in London at the Dominion Theatre on May 23. Jon's parents had flown into England to see their son triumph, but things went rather awry, when after thundering through 'Tokyo Road', the sound cut out as they entered into the riff for 'Get Ready'! Whether they had exceeded the officially-imposed limit on the PA decibel level - which would have enacted an automatic cut-off of the sound - or quite simply gremlins had gotten into the machinery no-one at the time was sure,

but there was a huge emptiness onstage. It only lasted a short time, before the sound came back and Richie carried on with his solo - and then the sound system gave out again! As the roadies desperately tried to put things to rights, Jon briefly left the stage, returning with a 12-string guitar in hand. Proclaiming to the audience, hands outstretched, that "I don't know any jokes, sorry," Jon proceeded to conduct a bloody singalong. Here was a man facing one of the most important, watershed gigs of his career (headlining in a city regarded as being among the three principle seats of influence in the music world - the others being New York and Los Angeles) and he's got no sound system at his disposal. Most performers, even seasoned professionals, would panic in a situation such as this. In fact, I have seen a number of top stars fail to turn such accidents to their advantage. But Jon simply reacted like a master.

He won over the capacity crowd with his bravura, and so successful had his singalong been that when the sound system buzzed back to life, he turned around and said: "No, I don't want the f**king PA!"
He took things a little further, by continuing with his strumming, before seemingly being coaxed back into 'Roulette' by the rest of the band.
If he had engineered and stage-managed the whole thing, Jon couldn't have done his reputation any more good. It was sheer genius. It also persuaded many of the industry big-wigs that they were truly dealing with somebody rather special.
As a result of the UK tour, the offer to appear at Donington arrived. In a later chapter I shall deal more fully not only with this performance on August 17, 1985, but also the band's return to the festival as headliners two years later. In '85, though, they were third on a bill lorded over by ZZ Top. Special Guests were the British progressive band Marillion. Below the Jovis were the fast-rising thrash heroes Metallica, Ratt (in Europe, even at their height, the LA rodents could never compete with Bon Jovi) and homespun English cult rockers Magnum.

It was a balanced bill, but the Jovis stole the day, even though their performance opened to the sound and sight of a pig's head thudding onto the stage. Whether this was designed to be a comment on the band, or was simply a symbol of approval one cannot say. But there was no sign of an adverse effect on the band's performance.

By the end of 1985, Bon Jovi hadn't achieved the big breakthrough so many had predicted and were waiting for. But they had moved a little further up the curve. '7800 Degrees Fahrenheit' took the band beyond a million units worldwide, which was a very healthy base.

And they were performing their own shows in certain key parts of the globe to increasingly receptive audiences. Perhaps David summed up the mood at the time rather well:

"With any band, you have to get the first pair of albums recorded and released as fast as possible, just to ensure you don't slip in the public's eyes. We did that, and then had more time for the third album, which was important. It meant we could write a lot more material and then have the luxury of picking our way through it before paring down the choice to the best numbers."

But the pressure was, to some extent, on Bon Jovi. They had to deliver third time out - or face critical mass and a possible nuclear explosion that would engulf them.

Faith and Glory

CHAPTER SIX

MANY A SLIP...

The relative disappointment of '7800...' left Bon Jovi in a rather difficult situation. Their profile, especially in a highly receptive Europe, was certainly on the move, but the failure to translate all the groundwork achieved on the 'Bon Jovi' record into something rather more tangible sales-wise clearly frustrated many of those involved with the band. Indeed, there were persistent rumours that the band were about to be dropped from the PolyGram family.

The veracity or otherwise of this statement has never been truly determined. Derek Shulman has always denied Bon Jovi were ever in danger of facing the axe. "No, it was certainly never considered by PolyGram as an option, at least not as far as I'm aware, he told me some years later. However, there were others convinced that Jon and boys were on the verge of the precipice. One man who claims to have been at least partially responsible for saving Bon Jovi from this fate is the British music entrepreneur Jonathan King.

Generally regarded as one of the most creative and ambitious people in the British music business, the all-powerful and ego-driven King alleges that he persuaded PolyGram that to drop the band would be folly.

He goes so far as to maintain that after Bon Jovi had broken big, he met them on a Concorde flight from New York to London when Jon personally thanked him for such a 'timely intervention'. Whatever, given the structure of record company philosophy and its attendant worship at the shrine of multi-platinum success, barely gaining a gold record for sales of half-a-million copies of '7800...' in America represented something of a flop for Bon Jovi, especially when you consider that the likes of Mötley Crüe, Ratt and others with obviously less musical dexterity were all selling at least twice than number of records. So, what to do?

The answer lay in a radical re-think of Bon Jovi's approach to the studio and recording. Lance Quinn was consigned to history and in came Canadian Bruce Fairbairn, resulting in a move from the relatively cloistered Warehouse Studios to the more cosmopolitan climes of Little Mountain Studios in Vancouver - Fortress Fairbairn.

Of course, with hindsight it seems a stroke of genius to work with someone of Fairbairn's stature, but at the time he first met Bon Jovi the quietly-spoken yet strong-willed Canuck was far from being a major name. He had gained success through the parochial attainments of such rock bands as Loverboy, Blue Öyster Cult, Honeymoon Suite, but remained a relative unknown - certainly not regarded as being in the league of, say, 'Mutt' Lange. This inevitably meant that he was cost-effective - and it is undoubtedly true that Fairbairn could perceive that Bon Jovi were on the verge of a huge breakthrough. Furthermore, what Fairbairn brought to Bon Jovi was an extra dimension of sound, rather necessary in Jon's view.

"Lance had too much work on his shoulders at the time. We needed something extra that Bruce could give us. I actually got to hear what Bruce could do, thanks to his work with (Geffen signed) Black 'N Blue. I liked the sound he got."

In addition, Bon Jovi also brought in Desmond Child as a co-writer for selected songs. At the time, Child was a relative unknown. He had gained something of a cult stature among aficionados of melodic rock thanks to his band Desmond Child & Rouge, but his reputation was far from made.

"There are those who believe that Desmond played an important part in breaking Bon Jovi," says Jon. "But they forget that at the time we worked with him for the first time, he wasn't that established. In all honesty, we helped him as much as he helped us."

There is no doubt that many people (although, strangely, not the band) involved with 'Slippery When Wet' knew when it was finished that they had a major album on their hands. But exactly how big nobody could predict. Jon took up residence at a rented apartment on the New Jersey shoreline with girlfriend (and future wife) Dorothea Hurley during the weeks preceding the album's release, and the band used this as a base to do a promotional round of interviews and photo shoots. There was an air of confident optimism about the five-piece as they prepared for the task ahead. Away from the pressures of the metropolis, Jon in particular seemed relaxed and primed.

However, despite the confidence oozing throughout the Bon Jovi camp, nobody could be prepared for what was going to happen. 'Slippery When Wet' was released in August of '86, and was to spend a total of 15 weeks in two bursts at the top of the US charts, peaking at Number Six in the UK. The LP was to sell in excess of thirteen million copies worldwide, thereby becoming one of the biggest-selling records of the '80s and doing much to establish melodic hard rock as a commercial force.

But what exactly caused the album to sell in such vast quantities? Certainly, PolyGram believed sufficiently in it to give it a huge marketing push. And the songs were of the highest quality. Desmond Child had given the band a lighter touch compared to previous albums, and Fairbairn's production gave the record a contemporary sound. But, whilst it was an excellent exposition of pop-rock, there was rather more to the album than mere superficial artistry. Indeed, this is why the album has not only endured during the intervening years, but has become established as a landmark release. RAW magazine in the UK rated it as one of the crucial releases of the '80s.

So, what is it about 'Slippery When Wet' that makes it such a popular album. Firstly, it has undeniable melodic quality. Songs such as 'You Give Love A Bad Name' and 'Livin' On A Prayer' were obvious and immediate candidates for radio play - the advent of Desmond Child had airbrushed some of the rougher edges out of the Bon Jovi songwriting technique. And the rapidity with which radio stations across the globe picked up on the music underlined the potency of the band's easy action tunefulness. But that is only the surface response. Beneath the surface, the album had a toughness and darkness that was not initially evident, but showed itself upon repeated exposure.

Jon himself felt at the time that the record was far more uptempo than '7800...'. However, if there was an absence of the moodier side of Bon Jovi this time around, nonetheless the lyrical aspect of the record amply displayed Jon's penchant for intelligent, sharp, analytical expositions. Even a song such as 'You Give Love...', the first hit off 'Slippery...', wasn't exactly a lovey-dovey, dewey-eyed love song. In fact, some of the verbiage had a barbed-wire slash to them: 'Your very first kiss was your first kiss goodbye'. Whether or not these lines were aimed at one of Jon's former girlfriends, actress Diane Lane, remains pure speculation. However, this opinion has been expressed by more than one person close to the singer. Whatever, few songs in the recent times have so perfectly captured the mood of jilted love as does 'You Give Love...'. How ironic that it became almost an anthem FOR lovers!

Elsewhere, 'Livin' On A Prayer', another of the best-remembered hits, has a blue-collared atmosphere than recalls Jon's hero Bruce Springsteen. Against a rhythmic salsa dip that proves insistent and irresistible, Jon croons about the struggle facing working class America in Reagan's 'brave new world'. Not a political song, or indeed an overtly social comment, the power of 'Livin'...' lies in the precise angst straining in every syllable. 'We've got to hold on to what we got/It doesn't make a difference if we make it or not/We've got each other...' pleads Jon. Like many of the most brilliant insights into the American psyche by such film makers as Frank Capra and Preston Sturges, it is precisely because he is not trying to score undergraduate socio-political points that Jon achieves in the course of one song something far closer to realism and the nature of human dignity than the likes of U2 could hope to present in an entire career.

Yet, because Jon has always been perceived as a 'pretty boy rocker', he has so far been denied the credibility and acclaim that his talents deserve. Jon's true artistry has always bubbled just beneath the surface, but it has also been there for anyone to discover. Maybe if he had been more prepared to indulge in pseudo-intellectual word games, he would have garnered more support from the hoi-poloi, but that has never been his way.

"I write what I feel," he says matter-of-factly. And what he feels is the touch of someone in sync with the American heartbeat.

But further into the album, we find 'Wanted: Dead Or Alive', which was, and remains, a hugely popular live attraction. The steady, chiming guitar whip from Richie cascades through the track with an epic urge, almost a desperate plea. And this is in keeping with the world-weary lyricism from Jon, as he espouses on life in a touring rock band. Jon's fascination with the cowboy theme is something that he has projected at every opportunity.

"I love the idea of cowboys roaming wherever they choose. And I feel that a modern rock band is very much the same. We do ride into town for a brief time, play our show before moving on to the next town."

Yet, 'Wanted...' isn't just another 'we are a rock'n'roll band. We take your women. We drink your booze. We trash your hotels' type of number. In feel and essence it has a certain relationship to the mighty westerns of the great film director John Ford, but also draws from the nihilist homilies of Sergio Leone and 'Shane', self-reliant, lone-riding icon of freedom and justice. The lyrical charm of 'Wanted...' is that it does possess a desperate edge. The glories of being in a rock band on tour are balanced against the tedium and the pain. 'You can tell the day by the bottle that you drink', wails Jon, in the process bringing to mind a line from AC/DC's 'Ride On', which has a similar theme.

Throughout the album Jon and the boys offer not only major musical muscle, but intricate arrangements and assured lyricism, which goes a long way towards explaining why the album became such a monster hit and has also endured. However, there were also other factors involved, ones that are not so easy to quantify, but nonetheless ones that also played a crucial role in breaking the band to such a huge extent.

Firstly, there was Jon's sex appeal. Naturally and acquisitively photogenic, he exuded a wholesome, matinee idol appeal that made him a hit with women of all ages. There was nothing threatening about Jon's image. Men felt comfortable with his attraction to women, whilst women themselves believed themselves able to fantasise about Jon without feeling undermined. He didn't exhibit the ambiguity of Jagger or Morrison, nor the decadence of Bowie or Mötley Crüe, nor the self-destructive wilfulness and libertine loutishness of James Dean or Axl Rose. No, there was, and is, a charm and innocence to Jon's appeal.

It meant that he could appear safely in the pages of such magazines as Smash Hits in the UK - teeny, pin-up pop papers. It meant that he could walk in any company. The same also applied, albeit to a lesser extent, to Richie Sambora. And the marketing nous of PolyGram and McGhee Entertainment ensured that this aspect was exploited. Nobody could dispute that by the end of 1986, Jon Bon Jovi was THE rock star pin-up. And sex appeal means record sales - an empirical formula that has proven correct through time immemorial. Mind you, Jon never felt entirely at ease with such a status.

The second factor that played its part in the promotion of Bon Jovi was what I would consider to be the 'Def Leppard Factor'.

There is no question that the release in 1983 of the multi-platinum 'Pyromania' album established a new regime in the history of melodic hard rock. Leppard became heroes, in particular throughout America. However, they had disappeared in 1985 to begin work on the follow-up album, 'Hysteria', which was not to be released until early 1987. Their absence left a void at the very highest level of the genre. Teenagers in the States, with a seemingly unrequited appetite for the sort of music Leppard had popularised, grabbed Bon Jovi to fill the vacuum. They were homegrown, available, pleasantly sexual and had a slew of strong songs to offer, as well as cleverly simple promotional videos, designed to show off the band's hugely ambitious live arena-filling presentation to the maximum extent.

It wasn't the first time that a US band had benefitted from the temporary absence of British heroes, and had used this to their advantage. Aerosmith achieved their exalted status in the mid-'70s when the Rolling Stones were out of the limelight. Styx, to some extent, used the unavailability of Yes to build a solid foundation for themselves.

In all of these cases, the US band who gained the breakthrough went on to underline their own individuality. But all of them needed that slice of luck and thereby responded to it. The same can be said of Bon Jovi.

So, add all these prime numbers together and what do you get? A big album, probably capable of selling one or two million copies, but not one that could sell more than five times that amount. One simply cannot legislate for such a huge album. Not quality of music nor weight of marketing expertise can possibly take any album to the dizzy realms enjoyed by 'Slippery When Wet'. As with Michael Jackson's 'Thriller', Prince's 'Purple Rain', Def Leppard's 'Hysteria' and Guns n' Roses' 'Appetite For Destruction', the trigger was the auto-momentum of the record itself. 'Slippery...' just took on its own life and blasted all opposition. Bon Jovi were much in demand on all fronts. The band whom Jon once described as "Just a bunch of ordinary guys from New Jersey" were now feted wherever they roamed.

But how would they cope with the pressure of acclaim and adulation? Ah, now there lies another chapter...

CHAPTER SEVEN

THE CONSEQUENCE OF FAME

The advent of fame is a strange beast indeed. It separates the men from the boys, the sane from the insane, the professional from the egomaniac. Fame has been known to drive some into their shells, to seek seclusion. It can push others into becoming drunk on the heady wine fermented in the glare of the spotlight, can seduce them into becoming junkies of publicity.

Few people are born into the reality of fame. For most, it arrives as a result of endeavour or achievement. It has always been fascinating to watch how various individuals - especially rock musicians - deal with the onrush of this most elusive of sprites.

I think it was Led Zeppelin's Robert Plant who once pointed out the salient fact that so many musicians spend the early part of their career courting publicity and media attention, but when they gain the success they covet, most musos then spend the rest of their career hiding from the media onslaught. Certainly, in my experience, this is close to being an irrevocable truism. Jon Bon Jovi, though, probably has the most balanced perspective on fame and how to deal with it that I have ever come across. He is at ease with himself and his position.

Jon isn't a controversial character by nature. He doesn't trash hotel rooms. He doesn't jump into bed with every passing groupie. Just about the only girlfriend he has ever had who can be called a 'celebrity' was 'Streets Of Fire' actress Diane Lane (prior to 'Slippery...' turning attention onto the singer and his band) - and that liaison not only proved very brief, but was courted more by the actress than Jon himself! No, Jon isn't one of life's spitfires. He gets on with the job in hand, alert to proceedings and openings and always keen to maintain the public persona of affability.

"I talk to fans in the back row when we're performing, and I have them sing something for me every night," Jon espoused during the lengthy 'Slippery When Wet' tour. "I point to members of the audience and talk directly to them because it's really important to keep that contact".

"If people come up to me and are real nice, I'll do anything - take pictures, sign autographs."

On a personal level, I recall meeting up with Jon during his promotional trek for the release in 1990 of the solo 'Young Guns II...' album. Jon was doing a succession of interviews in a suite hired for the occasion by PolyGram at one of the plushest hotels in New Jersey.

But Jon inevitably spent some time wandering around the bar area and also doing photo shoots in various outside locations on the shoreline. This being his home town, Jon literally couldn't wander around without being accosted by fans wanting autographs and pictures taken with him. He obliged everybody with a smile and a wave - unflappable.

"The way I look at it, these are the people who have put me up where I am today. They have bought the albums and concert tickets. Without them, where would Bon Jovi be? I feel it is part of my job to sign autographs and so forth."

Jon has also had to deal with having fans camp outside his home in New Jersey, something again he takes in his stride.

"When 'Slippery...' came out, it was very bad. There were kids camping in my parents' front garden! That was crazy. Now, it's died down quite a lot. There are always one or two fans hanging around outside. But so long as they don't cross the threshold and try to enter the house, then it doesn't bother me. In fact, I usually send somebody out from the house to make sure they are OK."

This relaxed attitude towards the fans obviously comes from Jon's own background, and the acknowledgement that it is a signal as to the attainment of position, the realisation of a dream.

Fame for Bon Jovi followed very quickly after the release of 'Slippery...'. At the time, the band were out on the road supporting southern rockers 38 Special in arenas across the US. It was akin to Billy Squier going out supporting Queen in the early '80s before he broke big, or Def Leppard in 1983 supporting Squier just prior to 'Pyromania' becoming a huge seller. It was perceived as no more than a warm-up - and a fail-safe. Should 'Slippery...' not have happened, then Bon Jovi were not committed to a costly headline tour of their own.

But of course 'Slippery...' did happen. And the rest is history, as they say. Bon Jovi became the byword for rock music across the world. They were acknowledged as the new masters of the form. But it also brought a change in attitude towards the band from those surrounding them.

One incident comes to mind when mentioning this. It came towards the end of 1986. Bon Jovi had just sold out 14 shows in the UK, beginning on November 7 at Bradford St.George's Hall ending with the fourth date at London's Hammersmith Odeon on November 25. To celebrate the enormous success achieved by the band, Phonogram Records (the UK label) elected to hold a major party for them at Break For The Border, one of London's top Mexican restaurants.

The assembled throng duly gathered for the festivities. And after a full hour, the stereo, which had been blasting out the sounds of various rock bands signed to the label, was suddenly turned up several notches as 'You Give Love A Bad Name' hammered its way over the system. Before anyone could attune themselves to the change in volume, the band made their way in through the door, literally surrounded by Phonogram personnel. These people were visibly pushing Jon away from the gathered celebrants towards a specific, enclosed VIP area, within which only selected invitees were to be allowed. The embarrassment on Jon's face was clear and obvious. He wanted to enjoy and savour this moment, to spend time and talk to people, including many who had been supportive of the band since their first visit here. But the powers-that-be were having none of it - they were determined to cloak their man in a veil of unapproachability.

Over the years, though, Jon has learnt how to handle situations such as this. He has balanced out the need to be seen as a star whilst also remaining approachable in a certain manner. His flair for media insight has been remarkable and astute.

Whilst Jon has consistently failed to set the gossip columns on fire, Richie has gained much attention, thanks to his associations with the likes of film star Ally Sheedy and the legendary Cher. For the most part, these have been harmless affairs that have certainly not damaged either him or the band. And Richie has also done much that is not publicly known for fans. One incident I feel is well worth recording.

It happened in the Summer of '89 when Bon Jovi were over in the UK for a headlining show at the Milton Keynes Bowl. One Bon Jovi fan was seriously ill in hospital, the Royal Free in London. When being told about the plight of the hapless fan and asked if he could possibly find time to talk to him, Richie did not hesitate. He got onto the phone and spent ages talking to the emotionally overwhelmed kid. It was a touching moment done with no thought about using this for cheap publicity. It was a simple act from a man who cares about his fans.

Bon Jovi have always been a band who have kept feet firmly planted on solid ground. They have never allowed awards or success to turn their heads. Moreover, they have steadfastly stayed fans of music and of personalities.

"I was invited to see the play 'Waiting For Godot' in New York just after 'Slippery When Wet' broke really big," recalls David Bryan. "I went backstage afterwards to meet the stars - including Robin Williams, who is one of my heroes. What's more I went to the bathroom, and there standing next to me having a piss was none other than the actor John Lithgow. He looked over to me and said: 'Hey, aren't you in that band Bon Jovi? My kids are big fans of yours'. Incidents like that make all the work worthwhile."

Meeting celebrities in various toiletry facilities across the globe is just one facet of the way in which Bon Jovi mix comfortably with stars from all walks of life. They are invited to celebrity parties at will, and are among the most photographed of all rock bands. Jon is always in demand.

Jon is also at ease in the company of celebrities. He is on first name terms with the likes of Elton John, film star Emilio Estevez and boxer Frank Bruno, to name but three. He has also used his celebrity status for charitable purposes. Gigs have been held in clubs and theatres on both sides of the atlantic in order to raise money for various organisations. In September 1992, for instance, the band played a one-off date at London's Astoria Theatre. It was a fun occasion, with Bon Jovi throwing in a number of favourite cover versions. The money raised was donated to the Nordoff-Robbins Foundation, "I told the record label that if I had to come over to do some promotion for the 'Keep The Faith' album then I wanted to do a gig like this."

And when the Mid-west of America was hit by flooding in the Summer of '93, the band donated the profits from various shows to flood relief organisations.

But one aspect of fame, as Jon found out during 1986, was the fact that it meant dealing with trivial questions from teeny magazines anxious only to tell the world what Jon's favourite colour was and when he last changed his socks, etc. Jon didn't take too kindly to such interviews, as he made clear on more than one occasions to interviewers. But, such is the price of being the most wanted musician on the planet.

Yet, whilst Jon was being approached by an ever widening number of publications - from the aforementioned teeny press to the more august journals and heavyweight TV programmes - he never forgot his rock roots. Thus, others in a similar position might have ignored those magazines who supported them they hit the gas pedal and roared into the rarefied atmosphere of fame and fortune. But Jon has never turned his back on those magazines. He has always been fully aware that his fan foundation lay principally within the rock market. He might now be acclaimed by a wider audience, and this might prove transient. Yet, as long as he stayed loyal to the rock genre - and was seen to be doing so - those fans would steadfastly remain loyal to him. A clever point, oft overlooked by others.

One other aspect of fame that clearly endeared itself to Jon was that people would take his opinions on other bands very seriously indeed. And he used this supposed power to good effect, in getting Philadelphia band Cinderella a recording contract with PolyGram.

"I saw Cinderella play at a club in Philadelphia and was really impressed with what I saw. Their vocalist, Tom Keifer, was particularly strong. So I persuaded Derek Shulman to go down and have a look at them."

The result was a record deal for the 'Rella, followed by much exposure courtesy of Bon jovi, both in terms of constant plugs in magazines and also crucial slots at key Bon Jovi shows. It's worth noting that Jon hadn't been the first top musician signed to PolyGram to see the potential and talent of Cinderella. Kiss bassist/vocalist Gene Simmons had spotted it earlier, but failed to get anyone to take him seriously - and had to give up on the band. Whether Jon had more clout, or whether Cinderella themselves had improved sufficiently since Simmons had seen them for a label to take a risk on them is a moot point. Whatever, there is no doubt that Jon used his own position and power to further the hopes and aspirations of another band.

"I feel it's my duty. I got help from people like Southside Johnny when I was starting out - and I was always grateful to them for that help. Now I am in a position to aid others, I would be neglecting my beliefs if I didn't do what can for them."

The other band whom Bon Jovi helped to find considerable success was Skid Row, fellow New Jersey residents. The story has often been repeated - and will be the subject of a later chapter - but Jon and Skid Row guitarist Dave 'Snake' Sabo were old school friends, both dreaming of the big time. When Jon found his niche, he didn't forget his old chum, constantly pushing them in interviews and eventually using his connections to get the band a management deal with McGhee Entertainment and thence a recording contract with Atlantic. And when the first Skid Row album was released in 1989, Bon Jovi gave them a further boost by taking them out on the road.

Relations between the two camps soured somewhat over alleged business dealings - which will be covered in more depth very shortly - but there is no question that Skid Row probably owe their career to the help they received from Bon Jovi.

But, for the most part, Bon Jovi spent 1986 and 1987 not engrossed in enjoying their new-found fame, but in touring, touring, touring. They traversed the world more than once, setting new attendance records at many venues. It was, in fact, almost a 'rock 'til you drop' trek that was with hindsight way too long and laborious. But Jon loved virtually every minute of it and he was, after all, the most in-demand rocker there was back then. The climax came in the UK in August 1987, when the band received the ultimate accolade - they were asked to headline at the prestigious Castle Donington Monsters Of Rock Festival - a truly momentous event worthy of its own chapter. So here goes...

CHAPTER EIGHT

LET'S DO THE MONSTER MASH

The Castle Donington Monsters Of Rock Festival in the East Midlands is one of the most prestigious hard rock/metal festivals of the British music calendar. Indeed, it could be argued that by the mid-'80s, it had become the premier event for rockers on a global level. Certainly, the invitation to headline this one-day event was a much coveted accolade. Bon Jovi received this particular salute in 1987, being contracted to headline at the eighth annual shebang on Saturday, August 22.

For Bon Jovi, it was a significant moment. Whilst the year-plus trek in support of 'Slippery When Wet' saw them traverse the whole planet, achieving much that was unique, nonetheless topping the bill at Donington proved something to the band and to the world; whatever their chart and pop success, they were still regarded as essentially a rock band. Others, Swedish band Europe come to mind, have made the mistake in the past of failing to balance rock foundations with popist hits, but Bon Jovi never had such a problem. The fans who had been with them since the start always remained dear to Jon's heart - and the reward of appearing at Donington showed that this commitment was reaping its due.

"It's the kids who've broken this band without a doubt," Jon told Kerrang!. "We really have come through the traditional ways. We're not an overnight sensation, we're a hard-working band with over 500 shows under our belts. It's always been a very honest thing, and people have responded to that."

Moreover, the announcement that Bon Jovi were to headline did not spark off a slew of protests as to why a 'pop' band were taking the pole position at the rock world's major event. The Jovis were accepted and acknowledged in rock circles. Contrast this with what had happened two years earlier with ZZ Top - amazingly there was an outburst of outrage by rock fans who perceived this most authentic of rock acts as a pop sell-out combo, because they'd got daytime radio airplay!

In taking this headlining role, Bon Jovi became the fourth band in the history of Donington to appear at the festival lower down the order one year, and thence to return two years later in a headlining capacity. They were also the first truly '80s band to top the bill and only the second all-American band, following in the wake of Rainbow (1980), AC/DC ('81/'84), Status Quo (`82), Whitesnake ('83 - they were second on the bill two years previously), ZZ Top (`85 - they were third two years earlier) and Ozzy Osbourne (`86 - he had played third on the bill in 1984). All of those acts had achieved their success in the late '60s or '70s. So, for Bon Jovi it was a remarkable accolade indeed, beating the likes of Def Leppard and Iron Maiden to the punch in dragging the festival into a contemporary format. What price would one have got in 1985 on the BJs headlining at Donington within two years? Long odds, I would venture to suggest.

For Jon and the boys, 1987 did indeed represent a return to the race track of Donington. In 1985, shortly after the release of `7800 Degrees Fahrenheit', the band's growing stature in the UK had been confirmed when they were slotted in third on a bill topped by ZZ Top, with special guests Marillion, fourth placed proto-thrashers Metallica, old sparring partners Ratt and openers Magnum.

The fivesome's sharp set that day had won them many new friends, stripped down to the basics and relying on music and rapport as opposed to gimmicks. Indeed, it could be argued that Bon Jovi were the band of the day on that sunny, bright afternoon of Saturday, August 17. Jon had also acquitted himself well in the promotional stakes, making himself readily available to all and sundry from the media. One amusing story, though, still sticks in the mind from that day.

The author, much the worse for wear after downing more than one pint of undiluted tequila (!), was backstage talking to another journalist who had been waiting patiently for Jon to appear to do an interview. In a fit of drink-induced bravado, the author volunteered to go and find Jon and 'remind' him of the waiting journalist. At the time, Jon himself was in his record company's hospitality tent 'meeting and greeting' various dignitaries. The author bounding into the tent, in true swashbuckling style, and without a thought for his own 'safety' or 'decorum' proceeded to tell Jon in no uncertain terms that: "There's a journalist backstage waiting to talk to you, she's been waiting for ages and unless you come right now the wrath of Doc Doom (the author's affectionate nickname at Kerrang! wherein he was employed back then) will descend upon you!"

The hazy reminiscence of that day leads me to conclude that most of record label executives gathered at the time were horrified by this outburst against their artist. Jon, however, thought it most amusing - and made his way to the waiting journalist, offering apologies for the delay. It was typical of the man - he took everything in his giant stride. Mind you, the sight of Jon the next morning at the breakfast table, shades in place, sitting next to Ratt guitarist Robbin Crosby and looking as if he'd burnt up the night with just a tad too much alcohol brought a smirk to a few faces - but at least he'd enjoyed himself and the occasion. Even then, Jon was confident that the band would return to Donington one day and headline.

"We'll make it, just you wait and see!" he said. Whether his confidence was truly heartfelt, or just media bravura who could tell - but back they came in 1987. And they were headlining.

Joining Bon Jovi on the bill all those years ago were special guests Dio (fronted by former Rainbow/Black Sabbath legend Ronnie James Dio), Metallica (like the Jovis, and indeed Dio, making their second trip to the festival), Anthrax (New York thrashers), W.A.S.P. (the Los Angeles shock rockers) and Cinderella (who had been taken very much under Jon's ample wing). The day attracted more than 50,000 fans to the site and was significant in that this was the year when Donington gained a wider clientele than hitherto had been the case. The denim'n'leather all-male brigade had been the bastion and spinal column of the festival's support up until that point, but Bon Jovi's chart profile and wider media interest meant that a number of most welcome females turned up for the show -although amusement and horror were caused in equal measure (depending on your viewpoint) when those clearly new to festival requirements came dressed as if attending a fashion show - stilettos and fancy clothing were hardly de rigueur for a festival notorious for its bad weather!

In the event, inevitably the heavens opened up just prior to Cinderella taking to the stage. The downpour turned the Donington open air 'grass auditorium' into an unwelcome mud bath. Fortunately, the rain ceased just before Cinderella took to the stage at 1pm, but the damage had been done - and much of the festival's bonhomie had been ruined.

Cinderella performed impressively that day. With a sound clarity that surprised many people, they displayed a clean-cut professionalism that was both authoritative and classy. Some, however, raised a few eyebrows at the fact that Cinderella had been blessed with such good sound quality - unusual for the opening band at a Monsters Of Rock Festival. Could it be that favouritism had been involved? Jon was to deny this at a later date.

"We certainly didn't manipulate anything to make Cinderella sound better than the rest. If they had a good sound engineer, then it was because they were being sensible. If the others couldn't find a good engineer of their own, then that's their problem. Don't blame us for that. We haven't given out any instructions about restricting the sound for any of the other bands."

W.A.S.P. didn't really need a strong sound. Their set relied somewhat on shock value, as they brought on 'Penthouse' editor Lindsey Drew and strapped her, topless and hooded, to a waiting rack, before mainman Blackie Lawless simulated whipping her. The effect was something of a gruesome pantomime - effective in its own tacky way, but not exactly a performance likely to set the damp festival on fire.

Anthrax, by contrast, relied on brutal musical attack, their brand of heaving, bleeding thrash bringing the crowd back to life, whilst Metallica, much heralded, suffered from the wetness of the day and a disembowelled sound. They never truly did themselves justice.

Thus, the stage was set for the headliners. The band made their arrival at the site in cars during the late afternoon, whilst helicopters flew overhead, acting as decoys for any fans waiting in ambush - an old trick, but an effective one. They were quickly ushered into their own enclosure, where security was strict. David Bryan's hopes of following his interest in soccer by attending a game at the local City Ground - home of Nottingham Forest - and only a few miles from the site - had failed to materialise in a welter of other commitments, but this disappointment apart, the band seemed in good shape and heart. However, Jon himself seemed tired and slightly listless.

Meeting him backstage before Bon Jovi took to the stage, there was little doubt that the sparkle had gone from his eyes and the spark from his voice. He seemed to be a mere shadow of the vital, vibrant individual I had encountered a year previously just prior to the band releasing 'Slippery When Wet'. Jon still had a keen interest in what was going on in the UK music-wise and what new bands he should be listening out for, but he certainly looked and acted like a man who needed a break, as he warmed up for the strenuous activity ahead on the Donington stage.

"I'm not the sort to just switch off and relax on a beach. It's not in my make-up. I'm a workaholic and I always feel like I have to be doing something constructive and useful," he said back then. Not much has changed in his outlook, except perhaps for an appreciation of the value of relaxation.

Whether writing songs for Jennifer Rush, Ted Nugent or Cher (as Jon and Richie had been doing. Following the success of 'Slippery...', the pair were very much in demand), or thinking ahead to the next Bon Jovi studio album, Jon didn't seem back then to be at ease. Like many workaholics, the satisfaction from achievement was offset by an inner frustration at the conclusion of a project. He was also a perfectionist, never happy with what he had done at any turn. Being a workaholic is a psychological timebomb, waiting to explode. Sooner or later, judgement is impaired. However, Jon was riding on the crest of a wave - and, maybe the panic of slipping off the mountain, made him determined to take advantage of all Bon Jovi had attained. Perhaps, before it slipped away. How much Jon was enjoying the success of the band towards the end of the 'Slippery...' world tour remains open for debate. But Donington was certainly to be the climax.

Indeed, the band gave their all, in another fine performance. However, the opening didn't exactly go as planned. Jon was supposed to slide down a rope onto the centre of the stage, as the band burst into life - the superhero's entry. The trick worked, but hardly anyone realised it had taken place - for the spotlight failed to pick out Jon on his descent stagewards. The best laid plans...

However, once into their stride, the band gave a memorable performance worthy of the occasion and their status as headliners. Jon put his tiredness behind him, drilled into shape by the surge of adrenalin that is the hallmark of all great performers. Even the slipping and sliding mud couldn't affect the buoyant atmosphere.

At encore time, Bon Jovi dragged on Twisted Sister vocalist Dee Snider and Iron Maiden's Bruce Dickinson to fulfil yet another tradition of the Jovi tour.

"We have an open invitation in most towns and cities we've been through. If any musician wants to get up and jam with us, then just bring along your instrument. It makes it more fun for us, and for the crowd," said Jon at the time. Dickinson took advantage of the occasion to tell the waiting throng in the mud that Maiden would be back next year to headline the event - even though no contracts had been signed at that juncture. But if this, and also the accidental death of a Brazilian fan who collapsed as he left the site (the band and festival organisers were in no way to blame), took the headlines in the media, nonetheless Bon Jovi had shown any sceptics left that they were still rocking out the hard way. Indeed, despite the fatigue of constant touring, the band seemed to be brighter than ever.

Bon Jovi were to tour for another three months (using the private jet they had been flying in since 'Slippery...' broke them into the big time). In all, the band had toured for some 16 months, played a total of more than 130 shows, accruing a gross income of over $28 million - truly staggering. And in the process, 'Slippery...' had gone on to touch nearly 18 million sales worldwide, thereby making it the biggest selling hard rock album of all time.

But I doubt whether Bon Jovi in general, and Jon in particular, had much greater satisfaction than headlining at Donington. The UK had been the first country to take them into their collective bosom. Now, they had been accorded the ultimate rock accolade - joining an elite club who have been capable of topping the bill at the most renowned festival in the world. So, what next? A long, langorous break in which to catch breath and take on real life once more? A trip to the launderette? A visit to the local fast food freak-out? Er, not quite. There was another album to do! Much to the surprise of everybody, Jon elected to jump pretty much straight into the recording of album number four. It was, with hindsight, something of a mistake.

CHAPTER NINE

BACK ON THE JERSEY TRAIL

Hardened gamblers would probably have put considerable fortunes on 1988 being a quiet year for Bon Jovi, with the five musicians using their recuperative powers to recharge drained energies. But this was not to be the case.

Much to almost everyone's surprise, the band returned to work after just a six week break, intent on making the most of their position. "We just felt strong enough and good enough to get back into the writing groove," says Jon. "Richie came over to my place every day and we sat in my bedroom and just wrote. In fact, by Christmas 1987 we had about 17 songs already demoed and ready to go."

The band then went into full rehearsal, with another dozen songs also being co-penned by the highly motivated Bon Jovi/Sambora partnership. The idea was to do a double album -a bold move, but one that Jon himself felt strongly about. The songs were good enough to carry the plan successfully into battle. However, other forces were to prevail and the album was eventually slated to be a single affair. Recording again took place in Vancouver with Bruce Fairbairn at the production helm. It had proven to be a formula that worked, so why change it? Jon himself, however, is sensitive to this day about accusations of 'using a formula'.

"We didn't start out the day before 'Slippery When Wet', you know? We were making records and playing in clubs for years before that. And as for all those accusations of 'finding a hit formula', well that was never our belief. We write what we feel. This is straight from the heart."

The album, when eventually finished, basked in the title of 'New Jersey'. Originally, the band were thinking of calling the record 'Sons Of Beaches'; they even went so far as to mock up a sleeve for the album, based on The Doors' 'Strange Days' album cover idea. It was a montage set on the Jersey shoreline, with the band included alongside a number of strange characters. It was the second time Bon Jovi were forced to scrap an album cover. It had happened on 'Slippery...' as well. The original design for that sleeve featured a close-up shot of the chest of a well-endowed young lady, barely covered by a skimpy T-shirt bearing the legend 'Slippery When Wet'. The design was to prove just a little too risqué for most markets, the album eventually being released with this sleeve only in Japan. The cover that was to adorn 'Slippery...' in most territories was to be a simple one, featuring the title scrawled on a black plastic bag covered with water!

Back in '88, 'Sons Of Beaches' metamorphosed into 'New Jersey', named after the state in which the band had grown up. The idea came to Jon from a patch he wore on his jacket during the 'Slippery...' tour.

"New Jersey is not a place, it's an attitude," Jon told RAW's Sylvie Simmons just after the record was released. "The attitude can be found in any town, wherever you're from. We're good buddies with Def Leppard and they've got that same outlook; they dig where they come from, they know what they do for a living, and they enjoy it, and that's the kind of approach you've got to have, no matter what your profession is, no matter whether you're from New Jersey or Iowa or Sheffield."

One thing the band were anxious to avoid was making a 'Slippery When Wet Part II', and they succeeded admirably in this task. The record came out in October of `88 and hit the top slot on both sides of the Atlantic. And, for the second time in succession, Bon Jovi had virtually allowed others to choose the track listing. On 'Slippery...', Jon had come up with the masterstroke of taking the tapes containing all the songs cut for the record down to a local pizza parlour in New Jersey...

"We just got in a load of kids hanging around, let them listen to the songs and let them choose which ones they felt worked best. After all, these are the sort of people whom we are making the record for, so why not let them choose for themselves?"

The same type of approach was taken with 'New Jersey'.

"We began by using Bruce Fairbairn's baby-sitters. They brought in a lot of their friends and we also pulled in some kids who were hanging around the studio. We got a cross-section of opinions from them, because some were fans, others hated us and there were a few who couldn't give a damn."

Bon Jovi simply sat them down, played the album and then heard the opinions. Whilst a clear departure from the usual scenario of allowing record company executives to decide what constitutes a good, all-round album, this again proved that Bon Jovi were determined to stay as close to their roots as was possible.

What the kids chose was a selection of songs as strong as anything the band had done thus far in their career. 'New Jersey' was a surprisingly positive and clean-cut record. If there was a sense of anxiety or tiredness about the band, it certainly didn't show up on the final product. Again, Fairbairn inspired a powerful, rich performance full of eddies and currents. And there were two choices that were not supposed to be on this record at all, but were being saved for future use, namely 'Stick To Your Guns' and 'Wild Is The Wind'.

"We were going to save them for the next album," says Richie. "But the kids we brought in to listen to the songs picked up on these two. Perhaps we wanted to do something a little different on this album, but these are the kids who will buy the record; they liked the emotional content of these songs. What matters aren't the songs themselves, but how you feel after you've heard them. Rock'n'roll should be more of an emotional release than a strict musical form, right?"

Right. And 'New Jersey' proceeded to emphasise the power of Bon Jovi. They were more than just 'another pop outfit'. there was longevity in their hearts, minds and music. The fear of following up the success of 'Slippery...', though, was clearly evident in the band's attitude and approach.

"We were scared shitless," admitted Jon at the time. "But you know what the great thing about success has been? Seeing how excited for us so many of our friends and fans have been. It's really amazing. It's almost as if our success has been their success as well. That's what drives this band on, just feeling the joy of the pleasure we have given to people. Maybe to some 'stars' it's the money, girls, power or whatever that proves to be their driving spirit. For me, the big prize is seeing how genuinely happy everybody is for us."

This philosophy allowed Bon Jovi to come to terms with the enormous, over-reaching success of 'Slippery...', put it behind them and get on with their lives. They simply refused to allow 'Slippery...' to dangle over them like a vinylised Sword Of Damocles.

So, what of the album? Opening with the tribal thud of 'Lay Your Hands On Me', it was clear that here was a record of maturity and guile. There was a healing quotient to the rhythmic mantra of the record, continued by the sophistication of 'Bad Medicine', the next track up and the first single to be released from 'New Jersey'.

A strange choice in many respects for a single, the accompanying video was also a departure for Bon Jovi - indeed, for anyone. Once again, the band put their trust in the fans. Basically, they gave out 150 video cameras to the fans invited along to the video shoot- and got them to film the clip! This was then mixed with live concert footage shot by a professional crew to give a different slant on the notion of filming a video. Unique indeed.

Moreover, the band played a 90-minute free show for those fans who came along to the video shoot, as a way of paying them back for patiently waiting through endless lip-synched takes. It was the band's first live date of 1988. Further in through the album came the wiry balance of 'Born To Be My Baby', a glorious, uptempo cadence, which betrayed a band in a jocular, delighted mood and the slightly sterner tones of 'Living In Sin', with its humble yet insistent beat. 'Blood On Blood' was very much a family affair, full of bold acclamation and the close ties born of Italian stock. Bon Jovi have always seen themselves as a close-knit family, with everything that entails, including arguments, major bust-ups, but always the loyalty and bond of 'belonging'. This was, perhaps, the first time those emotions had been so eloquently expressed in song.

Elsewhere 'Ride Cowboy Ride' again locked into Jon's fascination with the western theme, so brilliantly espoused on 'Wanted: Dead Or Alive', and 'I'll Be There For You' was a statement of intent and faith.

In all, the album showed Bon Jovi to be developing at an incredible rate. Not only did it contain the melodic elements that had made 'Slippery...' such a magnificent and crucial release, but it was inventive and stylised; not just a follow-up to what had gone before, this album took the band to a new musical level.

"In a way, what I wanted was to feel the high we attained with 'Slippery...' all over again," says Jon. "But with hindsight we didn't have enough time between albums. To do what we did was suicide, but the powers-that-be had us straight back out on the road as soon as we finished the record. That whole period was one through which we never seemed to be standing still. We put out 'New Jersey' and then toured and toured. It did burn us out. I remember being in Dublin at the RDS Hall (on October 31 1988 - the start of yet another world tour) and somebody said to me: 'What are you doing back here so soon?' I replied that this was rock'n'roll, and this was what it was all about and how much I loved the road. I meant it at the time as well. Only now can I actually appreciate how much I was chasing my own ass."

For Bon Jovi this was a watershed period in many respects. They had adulation, fame, money, power. But that was never going to be enough to satisfy Jon and his cohorts. What the singer in particular wanted was - RESPECT. He wanted to be seen as an artiste, not merely a pretty boy sideshow, doomed to 15 minutes of glory and then oblivion.

"I don't know if I have respect as a musician yet," Jon said back then. "But that's something very important to me. And I believe people are slowly coming to realise that Bon Jovi isn't gonna go away. We're here for the long haul."

The Bon Jovi 'New Jersey' tour opened up in Europe, trekking its way through Dublin (where Def Leppard's Joe Elliott joined the band onstage for an encore rendering of Thin Lizzy's 'The Boys Are Back In Town' - Lizzy were, and remain, one of Jon's personal faves), before heading to the mainland and dates in Glasgow, Birmingham, London. Four sold-out shows at the vast Wembley Arena in London proved that the band had more than kept the faithful with them - they had expanded on it. They were no longer a phenomenon, but a well-established rock band.

But, as the band grew, so it became increasingly obvious that Jon and Richie were becoming the focal point of attention. The others were being perceived in many quarters as also-rans. For the first time, Bon Jovi were being looked at by some people as being less a band and more a vehicle for the talents of Jon and Richie. Unfair, in many senses of the term, but perhaps inevitable. There were even rumours that Jon had threatened both Tico and Alec with the sack unless they lost some excess body fat - and that the pair had been despatched to undergo lipo-suction in order to pare down to fighting trim. Jon denies this allegation and also the fact that Bon Jovi had ceased to be a band and had become his own personal property.

"Just because the band bears my name doesn't mean it's me and backing musicians. Nothing could be further from the truth. We are a band in every sense of the term, OK? As for sending Tico and Alec to a health farm or whatever, no that's not the case."

As 1989 dawned, there was little doubt Bon Jovi were so well known that they simply couldn't move for fear of being mobbed. A long way removed from the situation just prior to the release of 'Slippery...' when Richie and Tico paid a visit to London's swank and trendy Limelight Club. The band were in town to appear on 'Top Of The Pops' (TV's premier weekly music show) just as 'You Give Love A Bad Name' was starting to break big. One girl, spotting Richie, asked him if he was in a band.

"Yeah," replied the guitarist.

"What are they called? Would I have heard of them?" asked the girl.

"The name's Bon Jovi?" came the response.

"Nah, never heard of you. Are you in a HEAVY METAL band? You look like you're in a HEAVY METAL band! I don't like HEAVY METAL."

Within a couple of years, nobody would need to be told who Richie and Bon Jovi were. Nor that they were not a HEAVY METAL band. 'New Jersey' had affirmed their place among the elite. But storm clouds were gathering, and the next couple of years, although augmenting the band's success, also brought trauma. It began with the arrest of manager Doc McGhee on charges of drug smuggling, and continued with amazing allegations from Skid Row. They were situations that threatened the hitherto tranquil existence of the New Jersey syndicate and brought a whole new meaning to Jon's statement that: "I run things like the Memphis Mafia."

The singer was referring to the close-knit community that was the Bon Jovi family. But others were to try and unfairly implicate Jon in shady dealings...

CHAPTER TEN

DOC IN THE DOCK

In April 1988, Doc McGhee had been arrested on charges of drug smuggling. Specifically, this referred to his role in the seizure six years previously of some 40,000 lbs of marijuana being smuggled into North Carolina from Columbia. It was an arrest that caused something of a shockwave through the rock music industry. However, for many it was merely the affirmation of what was already part of the gossip treadmill. McGhee's past had been rumoured about for a number of years.

McGhee himself was a flamboyant figure, always high profile and definitely a major force in the rock world by the time of his arrest. He was also the sort of person rock needed badly. We had become used by the end of the '80s to a succession of faceless paragons running the music industry. The days of Colonel Tom Parker, Brian Epstein, Andrew Loog Oldham and Peter Grant had disappeared. Lone swashbuckling adventurers were not the norm by 1988. Managers were accountants and lawyers, men of financial acumen with perhaps little interest in music. The same could be said of the people running the record companies. Teamwork and balance sheets were the order of the day.

Thus, somebody like McGhee who was a cavalier at heart was a welcome breath of fresh air in a stale, grey world. He brought humour and personality to his task, as he successfully guided first Mötley Crüe and then Bon Jovi to the heights. He had a reputation for enjoying himself and acting in a manner some would call 'irresponsible', yet others would maintain was simply in the tradition of those patricians who once ran the Hollywood film industry and also first established rock'n'roll. Stories are told about how he would go on the road with one of his bands in order to ensure the smooth running of operations, yet spend so much time partying that his partner, the more low-key Doug Thaler, would then have to follow in his footsteps to clear up not only any original problems on a tour, but also the ones left behind by Doc! Whatever the veracity of these stories, it is true to say that eventually the strain of working with Doc proved too much for the hapless Thaler; he dissolved the partnership with McGhee, taking Mötley Crüe with him, whilst Doc remained overseeing Bon Jovi's affairs.

McGhee himself had been involved in music through various guises (including that of a promoter) before really throwing himself into management firstly with the Mötleys and thence with Bon Jovi. True, he had once managed Canadian guitarist Pat Travers, but his introduction to long-term successful management only really came with the acquisition of these two acts. His previous drug connections had been talked about - perhaps more accurately, whispered about - in rock circles for some little while after his elevation to the upper echelons of managerial status. Some believed he had been a frontman for the Mafia -and still remained so. Others believed he had got involved in drug running during his early days in order to finance McGhee Entertainment. Whatever, the upshot was that few people were shocked or surprised by his eventual arrest and subsequent conviction. However, a darker, more sinister question was raised in many people's mind: Did Jon and the band know anything about Doc's drug connections?

Nobody seriously felt that Jon was in any way involved in any drug smuggling that might have taken place. The original offence had, after all, occurred in 1982, before Bon Jovi had even met up with Doc and subsequently signed to his organisation. And all the evidence suggests that McGhee had given up all interests in such illicit activity before throwing himself wholeheartedly into rock management. But could Jon have known about Doc's shady past, and if so did he just choose to turn a blind eye to it? That in itself is a difficult question to answer. Jon's attitude towards drugs has often been documented. Indeed, back in 1987 he had taken part in the Rock Against Drugs campaign, wherein a number of major luminaries participated in making commercials screened by the likes of MTV in America. Jon shot his commercial inbetween his busy touring schedule.

"I think this is a very important thing to do," said Jon at the time. "I put in time last year and felt great about the results. I see a lot of kids in my travels. Most of them don't know what they're doing with their lives. I can understand where they're from. I've been there myself. I don't want to sound like I'm preaching or anything. I just want to share my experiences."

"When I was very young, I used to do a lot of drugs. It started out with just drinking beer at High School, and you puff on a joint. But then one night I must have smoked some bad pot or something. Anyway, I felt really sick and it took me ages to shake the feeling off. Honestly, I kept hallucinating. It was awful. In the end I was rushed to hospital by the parents of a friend. I haven't touched anything since. That experience taught me a lesson."

Given this commitment, I find it hard to believe that Jon would ever condone his own manager's involvement in drug smuggling, which leads me to the conclusion that he had no idea about Doc's past in this respect. However, it also must be borne in mind that Jon himself would undoubtedly have gone into McGhee's past very carefully before agreeing to sign with him in the first place. All of which would lead one to assume that something about such illegal activity must have come to light. So, there is a school of thought that suggests that he did know about Doc's past - and chose to ignore such misdemeanours, in the certain knowledge that the man was no longer involved in such activities and was the best choice to manage the band.

Does this latter theory hold up? Personally I doubt it. These were, after all, no more than unsubstantiated stories at the time, and if Jon had heard them he would probably have given Doc the benefit of the doubt. But, once McGhee was arrested, what was Jon to do? On the one hand, he could stand by his friend and business associate, and thereby risk being accused of tacitly supporting Doc's drug smuggling past - in the process undoing much of the good he had been seen to do in exposing the dangers of drug taking. On the other hand, he could distance himself and the band from Doc, perhaps even sever the contractual connections, and thence stick to his principles over drugs - but in the process his strong commitment to seeing Bon Jovi as a family would be broken for good. A family stands by each other, even in times of stress and strain.

Ultimately, Jon chose to stick by Doc in his hour of need. By issuing such a statement, Jon in no way condoned what his harassed manager had done in the past, but made it clear that he himself saw no reason to vilify him further. It was a brave move - many felt the softer option would have been to fire Doc, but Jon has never been one to take the easy way out if he felt it wasn't ethically right.

Eventually, McGhee was convicted for his part in the drug offence. but to the amazement of many, his sentence was a rather lightweight $15,000 fine, a five-year suspended prison term and community service, which included having to set up a foundation to fight drug abuse, which was called 'The Make A Difference Foundation'. For the second time, the McGhee organisation had been involved controversially in apparently turning the American judicial system into something of a joke. In 1984, Mötley Crüe vocalist Vince Neil was arrested after crashing his car whilst intoxicated on a Los Angeles freeway, in the process killing passenger Razzle, drummer with Hanoi Rocks. He was charged with vehicular manslaughter, but after much plea bargaining, got off with a sentence of community service, which included several commercials warning impressionable youngsters about the dangers of driving whilst under the influence of alcohol.

BON JOVI

In both cases, there was outrage in many quarters at the seemingly insubstantial sentencing. However, it could also be argued that imprisoning either party would not have taken advantage of their unique position to influence others to avoid the traps into which they had fallen. Seeing Vince Neil telling kids not to get in a car and drive away whilst intoxicated might well have had more effect than any other form of advertising. The same could be said for McGhee. He was sentenced to raising money for the 'Make A Difference Foundation', dedicated to fighting the battle against drug abuse.

Frith And Glory

McGhee chose to fulfil his sentence whilst at the same time cleverly raising his own bands' profiles in Russia, a country beginning to gain exposure to the ways of the western world - and a potential goldmine for rock music in future years. McGhee organised the two-day Moscow Music Peace Festival on August 12/13 1989 at the Olympic Lenin Stadium, wherein Bon Jovi and Mötley Crüe were joined by Skid Row (another part of the McGhee family), Ozzy Osbourne, the Scorpions, Cinderella, Russians Gorky Park and several other local acts. But this festival itself was to be wracked by controversy - especially over billing.

The idea put forward was that nobody would really be headlining. But Mötley Crüe immediately objected to having to go onstage before Ozzy Osbourne, thereby precipitating a row that nearly ended with Ozzy boarding a plane and leaving the country before the first gig! Moreover, Mötley (again!) objected to Bon Jovi not only closing the show but also being the only band on the bill to use pyrotechnics. It was a sign of the strain between the two bands at the time, and perhaps one could understand all of this frustration suddenly coming to the boil. When Bon Jovi had first started out, Mötley were already major news. But the Los Angeles band had effectively stood still, whilst the Jovis had gone on to achieve enormous acclaim and success. Whatever, by the time of the Moscow Music Peace Festival, Bon Jovi were by far the bigger attraction. Jon, though, was always careful to try and avoid any confrontation. Talking at the time he said: "I think to call us headliners just because we had use of pyros was all wrong. It wasn't like that at all. And nobody else was banned from using them. It just made sense because we were playing in the dark."

Whatever, there was a fisticuff altercation between Mötley drummer Tommy Lee and Doc McGhee during Bon Jovi's set on the first day. There was certainly, little sign of 'Peace' at this festival. McGhee himself seemed to see the festival less as a penance and more of the affirmation of his own pre-eminent position within rock music. More than one eye witness attested to his arrogant strutting attitude throughout the visit to Moscow, even at one point being heard to proclaim: "It's a big world out there, and half of it is mine!"

Maybe, the advent of the Moscow Festival put the first nail into the coffin of the relationship between Jon and Doc. Whatever, there were signs of strain between the two. Although Jon has sedulously avoided criticism of Doc, more than one person confirms that Jon held the opinion in the wake of Moscow that, to some extent, Bon Jovi had been used by their manager. Away from the controversy, Jon told Phil Alexander of RAW his opinion on Russia, having paid this fleeting visit: "I see Russia opening up and I can see why they're opening. There's this country where the military defences are one of the best in the world, but they can't build a fucking blender. They've realised that when they built those walls around themselves, they cut off their learning processes too. The rest of the world has passed them by and they can't feed their own people because there's no money there. Money makes the world go round and the Russians have realised that, so they're gonna tumble those walls to make some."

"They're gonna open the gates and everybody's gonna leave and the West'll move in there. The West is just dying to rip these people off! They've found out (in Russia) that Communism is a nice theory but it's shitty in practice."

But Jon was also impressed with the Russian spirit of rock'n'roll. "I always thought that the country would be like the film 'Red Dawn', and would be very alien in its attitude. But what you learnt the more you travel is that there is not really much difference between people, and everybody enjoys rock'n'roll music, don't they?"

Just prior to visiting Russia, Bon Jovi had themselves received a taste of what it meant to release an album there. They had signed a deal with the Melodiya label and received the princely sum of $9,600 for the licensing of the 'New Jersey' album - not exactly riches in abundance.

The 'profits' from the Moscow Music Peace Festival were donated to the 'Make A Difference Foundation' - although precisely how much this was still remains slightly clouded. Some felt Doc McGhee used the ambiguous phraseology attending the term 'profits' to ensure that all of his bands came out with money in their pocket from the trip. Jon hotly denies this: "All the money was donated to the cause. We made nothing from the trip - in fact, we lost out, if anything."

In addition, a compilation album was put together called 'Stairway To Heaven/Highway To Hell', wherein cover versions were undertaken by the likes of Bon Jovi, Mötley Crüe and Skid Row of songs associated with rock stars who had met untimely deaths. The Jovis chose to honour the late, great Phil Lynott by covering Thin Lizzy's 'The Boys Are Back In Town', long a staple of the band's live set.

"I am a massive Lizzy fan," exclaims Jon. "Phil Lynott was a genius, his songs are amazing. I just wish that those who surrounded Phil when he was really badly hooked on heroin would have taken him in hand and just spoken to him. It could have made a difference. I'm not saying it would have been an easy thing to do, but it could have saved a brilliant musician and a human being from throwing away his life."

Also involved on the album were the Russians Gorky Park, who covered The Who's 'My Generation' in honour of drummer Keith Moon. They were to become more closely associated with Bon Jovi when Jon and Richie co-wrote the song 'Peace In Our Time' for them, and then played on the recorded version (to be found on their self-titled debut album from 1989).

In all, this period was to prove a strange one for Bon Jovi. The whole Doc McGhee incident had given them unwanted publicity, and Jon himself was arrested in March 1989 after staggering onto the Wollman Ice Skating Rink in New York City at 3.30 am. He was picked up for trespassing with girlfriend Dorothea Hurley and a couple of people from the McGhee office. It was all harmless japery, but made the front page news - such was interest in the man. That very same month, ironically, the mayor of New York declared a Bon Jovi Day in honour of what the band had achieved, in the process giving them the keys to the city!

As if all of this wasn't enough, Jon finally married long-time sweetheart Dorothea on April 29, 1989 at the Graceland Chapel in Las Vegas. But it was to be Skid Row who cast the next giant shadow over Bon Jovi, and in process created a controversy raging to this day.

CHAPTER ELEVEN

ON THE SKIDS

*T*here is an old adage worth repeating here that you should never go into business with friends - the result is almost always acrimonious! Jon Bon Jovi found out just how true this saying was when he got heavily involved with Skid Row. Mind you, it all started out so smoothly and well.

Skid Row are a New Jersey band as, of course, are Bon Jovi. They feature guitarist Dave 'Snake' Sabo, who not only is an old school chum of Jon's but, as already stated, played with Jon in one of his early bands, namely the precursor to Bon Jovi called The Wild Ones - indeed, you'll recall 'Snake' was actually replaced by Richie Sambora, as at the time he neither had the technique nor application to make it in the big time where Jon was determined to head.

But Jon always kept in touch with 'Snake', and when the latter put together his own band, Skid Row, Jon took an active interest in proceedings. The guitarist found like-minded personnel in bassist Rachel Bolan, guitarist Scotti Hill, drummer Rob Affuso and Canadian wildman singer Sebastian Bach. They began gigging and by 1986 seemed to have a future on their hands. Certainly Jon thought so. He took time out during the promotional stint for 'Slippery When Wet' to extol the virtues of his friend's band:

"They are one of the most exciting young bands that I've seen recently. And I am doing what I can to help them along.
I genuinely believe they can go a long way in this business."

Praise indeed. And Jon went considerably further in his quest to promote Skid Row. He persuaded Doc McGhee to sign them up to his company for management, and thence they received a recording contract from Atlantic Records. When their self-titled, debut album came out in early 1989, Jon was right on hand to support the band in any way he could. The Skids were taken out as the opening act on the Bon Jovi 'New Jersey' US arena tour, and were introduced to British audiences when the Jovis headlined a one-off date at the Milton Keynes Bowl in the Summer of '89. It is certainly true to say that, whilst Skid Row might have made it big without help from Jon Bon Jovi, nonetheless that sort of support did them no harm at all.

But suddenly, things turned sour in this seemingly idyllic relationship. Rumours started to spread that Skid Row had unwittingly signed a contract whereby Jon and Richie made all the money accruing to the band through their music publishing, which in the case of a band as successful as Skid Row could amount to millions of dollars. It was further suggested that when the Skids found out about it, they freaked out - in particular Sebastian. As a consequence, the singer even went missing for a time, with stories circulating that he was all set to quit Skid Row and join Guns n' Roses, who themselves were going through one of their many traumas with Axl Rose! Of course that proved to be nothing more than fanciful rhetoric, but there seemed to be something to the story of contractual controversy. It was a story that simply refused to go away.

Then in November 1990, I received a call from an irate Sebastian, at home in New Jersey. He was, to say the least, furious. He had been reading interviews with Jon done to promote his forthcoming first solo album, 'Blaze Of Glory: Music From The Soundtrack Of Young Guns II'. During the course of several interviews, including one with the author, he had intimated that he had come to blows with Sebastian whilst Skid Row were supporting Bon Jovi in the US.

"Things got to such a point that, in the end, I knocked him onto his little butt. But then I picked him up and hugged him. He was just being too arrogant for his own good. Something had to be done about it," was the way in which Jon put it. No big deal made about it, but it had an impact in the Bach home.

Sebastian hotly denied ever being punched by Jon. Furthermore, he claimed that although Jon had confronted him, it had been in the company of several others.

"Jon had his brother and several bodyguards with him," insisted Sebastian. "He got them to pin me against a wall, and then threatened me. He stood there wagging his finger and lecturing. Well, I was quite prepared to take him on, but not with the others with him. So, I told him that if he wanted to step into a room by himself, then I would have punched him out. No problem. Who do you think would have won? A lightweight Bruce Springsteen fan or a heavyweight Metallica maniac like me."

The rant went on for quite some time, with Sebastian threatening all manner of retribution on Jon when their paths cross again. But in the midst of this tirade, Sebastian openly attacked Jon for "stealing from Skid Row". The singer finally came out in public and accused Jon of "ripping off money that rightfully belonged to Skid Row. He has $70 million in his bank account, but he seems to be desperate to get an extra $2 million from us. Why, I don't know. But he has us under a publishing contract whereby we make nothing at all. And I promise you that unless things change we will not carry on. I'd rather split this band up than carry on making money for Jon Bon Jovi".

The cat was definitely among the pigeons. The truth, it seemed, was out. What made it seem even worse was the claim that Richie, also part of this agreement, had been embarrassed by the situation and had thus handed back the money he had made to Skid Row.

"What happened was that I was part of a company with Jon, but disagreed with what was going on. So, I gave back some money and got out."

That was how Richie summed up his part in the delicate situation. But the question remained: Just what had gone on? Did Jon, in collusion with Doc McGhee, coerce Skid Row into a signing that was illegal or unethical? Perhaps the truth is a little more complicated and certainly doesn't leave Jon as vulnerable to blatant accusations of unfair practice. So, let's go back a little.

When Bon Jovi took Cinderella under their wing, it was done with no financial reward - nor any thought thereof. But, it has to be said that Jon's role in the whole Cinderella process was little different to that of an A&R man cum publicity agent. And had he been employed in either of these two capacities, then he would have made a healthy sum of money from the band's success. But he chose not to pursue this avenue. However, when it came to Skid Row, Jon clearly decided to put the whole situation on a more professional basis. It was a delicate problem, but one that had to be tackled.

Dealing with friends is difficult enough when it comes to professional pursuits. Often things are taken for granted. By putting their PROFESSIONAL relationship on a contractual and formal basis, Jon was ensuring 'Snake' never felt he was accepting a charitable offering from an old friend - and also maintaining his own equilibrium. But there was more to it than that. Just why was a contract signed that seemingly gave Jon (and Richie at first) complete control over Skid Row's publishing finances - and surely the Skids must have known what they were giving away?

The answer to the first part remains known only to Jon. But, one must wonder as to how much input he had in the making of that platinum 'Skid Row' album. Various members of Bon Jovi went down to the studio (Royal Recorders in Lake Geneva, Wisconsin) to hear what was being done, and also to lend advice. It is my contention, though, that Jon was a lot more involved than he has ever admitted. For instance, despite denials from all quarters, I can't help but feel that Jon wrote the song '18 & Life', the Skids' first big hit and the song that effectively broke them, first in the US and then worldwide.

Faith and Glory

And
ory

Without the impact of '18 & Life', it is doubtful whether Skid Row could have sold so many albums. What makes me feel this way? Simple. You only have to listen to it. '18 & Life', both lyrically and musically, is completely out of synch with the rest of the hard-hitting 'Skid Row' album. It is delicate, mature and blessed with a certain honesty and articulacy of emotion that was the hallmark at the time of Jon and Richie. It could easily have slotted onto the 'New Jersey' album, and I can't help but wonder if indeed it was originally penned for that very record.

Jon himself has always denied he ever got involved in Skid Row's songwriting. But, if he had been heavily involved in writing this number, a few things become clearer. By giving away a cast-iron hit to aid Skid Row, Jon ensured that this band would break through. But why should he dump a money-spinner without earning anything himself? By securing the publishing royalties on that first Skid Row album, Jon would have been making back the money he himself could have earned by keeping it for a Bon Jovi album. What's more, its success triggered off a financial windfall for Skid Row in other areas - one they couldn't have reaped without the success of '18 & Life'.

This theory won't be popular with Skid Row, and it might embarrass Jon to some extent, but it is one I hold to. But, leaving aside this particular analysis, other questions must be faced. If Skid Row were signing away their publishing royalties, it must have been done with the full knowledge of their management - McGhee Entertainment. Did Doc McGhee mislead Skid Row, and fail to explain to them fully what they were signing? If so, he would have been guilty of gross professional misconduct. So, why is it that the band have remained with him for management, even after the controversy broke worldwide? Surely, it would have made sense for Skid Row to sack McGhee and take legal action against him for failing to fulfil his part of a management contract. Unless...

Unless Skid Row did indeed know what they were signing away. Or, at least, unless certain key members in the band took the decision that it was worth signing away this part of their income in order to secure the total backing of Jon Bon Jovi and of '18 & Life'. Unless, perhaps Dave 'Snake' Sabo knew precisely what he was doing.

Before going any further, let me say unequivocally that I do for one minute believe that Dave 'Snake' Sabo did a secret deal with Jon, not Bon Jovi, whereby he made money from Skid Row without the others knowing - far from it. I just believe that 'Snake' was consciously prepared to take a calculated risk in signing away a certain percentage of potential income to Jon in exchange for his patronage. Nothing else makes sense, does it? For, if you take the view that Skid Row did not know what they were giving away contractually, then firstly, one has to think them dumb and stupid (not the case) to fail to read their contract and also not to get independent legal advice, and secondly, you have to accuse
Doc McGhee of betraying the best interests of his client (and Skid Row were as much his clients as Bon Jovi). In the latter case, legal action would surely have been the result.

No I feel 'Snake' at least knew exactly what he was giving up. Moreover, let's also remember that in order to extricate Sebastian from a previous managerial contract Jon put up $10,000. And in how many other ways did Jon aid Skid Row financially in their early days? To accuse Jon as Sebastian did was grossly unfair - and also perhaps untrue. Even when Richie handed back his share of the money, it wasn't done because he felt that it was wrong, but simply because he didn't want to deal with the embarrassment. At no time did Richie accuse Jon of wrongdoing.

Furthermore, if there had been a case for stating that Jon was guilty of unethical behaviour, why is that 'Snake' has remained on such good terms with him? Friends are not known to maintain their relationship if one feels that the other has grievously harmed him, whether physically or financially.

And when the question was put to 'Snake' as to how he had reacted to Sebastian's outbursts, 'Snake' was careful not to suggest that he agreed with the singer's accusations about financial impropriety. Continuing this theme, if Sebastian was expressing the Skid Row line, why is that he made his verbal attack without the prior knowledge of the rest of the band? And why didn't the other four guys jump in on his side? I believe that Sebastian was offering an honestly felt opinion, but wasn't aware himself of some of the dealings within his own band.

Inevitably, the controversial publishing contract was amended to ensure that the Skids got their due from future recordings - and, if as was claimed, the agreement was for Jon to receive all of Skid Row's publishing monies in perpetuity, then there is a case for suggesting a little greed came into it. But, I stress, IF that was the case.

But, relations between Jon and Sebastian have remained entirely strained. What was the truth about the alleged fight? Did Jon punch out Sebastian? Or did he accost the Skid Row singer whilst in the company of security men, rather than face him on his own? Only a few people know the truth about it, and they are not talking.

Sebastian is brutally honest about himself and everyone else - and would I am sure have admitted to being struck out by Jon. So, why did Jon mislead (if indeed he did)? The simple and straight answer is that perhaps Jon felt threatened by the situation. Relations between Jon and Sebastian had become difficult on the tour - the latter is a hard man to deal with -and whilst it is perhaps true that no blows were exchanged, Jon may have felt that since he verbally floored Sebastian, the effect was the same as if he had really landed a punch or two. Yes, you can accuse me of copping out and trying to make Jon look better in the situation than was really the case, but you don't blatantly lie during interviews if you know that there is every danger of being exposed as a liar by a second party. Jon must have known that Sebastian wouldn't take such a claim lying down (if you'll pardon the expression), so I feel that he perhaps confused his language somewhat, but was mainly talking about a metaphorical fight. That's my story and I'm sticking to it!

Whatever, there is still to this day bad blood between the parties concerned. Jon and Sebastian are still in a state of strain, with the latter's constant references to New Jersey as "Bon Jersey" not exactly helping matters. But, the singer has also never tried to hide the fact that Bon Jovi played a crucial role in breaking Skid Row.

"Some people think that I caused this fuss because I didn't appreciate what he (Jon) had done for us," Sebastian told RAW's Dave Ling in June 1991. "The point is that I appreciated it so much that we gave him more money that the rest of the guys in the band put together!"

One can't help but wonder if Jon ever regrets the help he gave to Skid Row. It has ended up nearly ruining his reputation - and to this day, there is still no definitive viewpoint on what precisely happened, both physically and contractually, between the two camps. Much of the above is speculation based on information gleaned over the past couple of years and also on intuitive insight. How ironic, though, it is that Bon Jovi were to leave the McGhee organisation, whilst Skid Row remained.

If the Skid Row controversy threw a little dampener on progress within the Bon Jovi camp, there can be no doubt that the next period in their development was to further fuel the fire that the band were on the verge of breaking up. For Jon elected to do a solo album, and then Richie followed suit, as did David.

Could Bon Jovi survive this hiatus? Was this really the end?
Only time would tell. In the meantime, Jon donned his cowboy boots and headed out on the plains....

CHAPTER TWELVE

GOING SOLO

Bon Jovi were in need of a rest after the rigours of practically five years without any sign of a break. They had worked hard to establish themselves and once they'd broken into the big time, they suddenly found themselves in a constant state of demand. The 'New Jersey' tour alone amounted to 237 shows in just 16 months. An incredible work-rate that few bands would even attempt. But such was Bon Jovi's attitude and dedication. They had finally succeeded in headlining at Giants Stadium in New Jersey (home of Jon's beloved American football team the New York Giants), which was the realisation of a dream come true. They had returned to the UK to play at Milton Keynes Bowl alongside Europe, Skid Row and Vixen.

"Well, we had thought of trying to play at Wembley Stadium instead of Milton Keynes, but a band called Bros (transient pop stars) were booked in there. We were determined, though, to do our own thing, and not to go back to Donington or some such place. This was to be our gig. I remember flying up to the Bowl. We passed over Wembley Stadium on the way, and there were not a lot of people there. We did better business. It was gratifying to know that even up against one of the trendiest of chart bands we could still prove to be a better crowd puller!"

That day was to be a special occasion for Bon Jovi, August 18 1989. There was no Donington that year because of problems in 1988 (two fans died tragically on the site during a set by Guns n' Roses), so hard rock fans were starved for open air action. Bon Jovi provided that in abundance. With Aerosmith singer Steven Tyler and guitarist Joe Perry joining the Jovis for a run-through of the 'Smiths classic 'Walk This Way' at encore time, there was a truly festive atmosphere. Once again, the drawing power of Bon Jovi was unequivocal.

Later that year came a long-form video called 'New Jersey - The Videos', a collection of seven tracks (two versions of 'Bad Medicine', plus 'Born To Be My Baby', 'I'll Be There For You', 'Lay Your Hands On Me', 'Blood On Blood' and 'Living In Sin'), plus interviews and home movie footage. Jon described the collection thus:

"You've heard about around the world in a day. Well, it's been 455 days and three times around on 'The Jersey Syndicate Tour'. These are the videos that helped spread the word worldwide."

In addition, the video for 'Lay Your Hands On Me' was donated to the charity long-form video released to raise money for the beleaguered, earthquake devastated region of Armenia. But now was the time to take a breather, to step back from the whirlpool of activity and plot ahead into the '90s. Now, surely, was the time for Bon Jovi to put everything on ice. Jon could put his feet up and enjoy the harvest he had deservedly earned. Er, well that was the theory. In practise, Jon did put Bon Jovi temporarily into the closet. But he certainly didn't halt activities in the slightest. There was a solo album to do and also a record label to set up.

Jon is a restive figure, seemingly incapable of standing still for long. As I've mentioned before, he is a workaholic, constantly getting involved in projects, be it as a songwriter, producer or performer. But now he put his tireless energies into two fresh dimensions.

Firstly, he got involved in putting together a solo album for the Vertigo label. Well, to call it a solo album was perhaps being a little loose with definitions. In fact, it was more a soundtrack for the film 'Young Guns II'. The first film had become something of a bratpack western special, starring the likes of Emilio Estevez and Keifer Sutherland. It had been a huge commercial success and inevitably led to a follow-up, once again starring many of the hottest young talents in Hollywood. And who better to approach to provide the music for this extravaganza than a hot-shot rocker who had always seen himself as something of a cowboy - Jon Bon Jovi.

Jon eagerly accepted this project. It was perhaps the greatest challenge of his career. He was out on his own. Moreover, he would stand or fall by his own talents and perceptions. Even restricted by having the subject matter of the album already defined, Jon positively glowed and basked in the opportunity.

"Sure, I had to watch the film and make the songs fit in, which meant that it's not really a solo album in the strictest sense of the term. But I found the whole experience very rewarding indeed. It also gave me a chance to work with a lot of other people, like Elton John and Jeff Beck, the sort of talents whom I could dream about collaborating with when I first started out. Honestly, you cannot imagine what it meant to me to be able to do this."

The album was written by Jon, who also produced it himself in association with Danny Kortchmar, and the music was blessed with the unmistakable stroke of genius. Inevitably, it had the scent of Bon Jovi in its nostrils, but Jon had the ability and openings to take the sound and style further on up the hill.

The big hit was the title track, 'Blaze Of Glory', with its winging guitar chimes and feel of open space, emphasised by the accompanying video. But that just the tip of the iceberg. The likes of the heaving 'Billy Get Your Guns', the more distraught 'Miracle', the furious 'Justice In The Barrel', the anthemic 'Dyin' Ain't Much Of A Livin'' and the cinemascopic vision of 'Santa Fe' are all masterstrokes. The last-named in particular was among the finest songs of Jon's career thus far.

"Yeah, I would have to say that 'Sante Fe' is my favourite cut on the album. But you know what? It's very strange having success as a solo artist when you're so used to sharing it with a band. There is an unusual feeling of loneliness that's hard to describe."

'Blaze Of Glory' was indeed a huge success story. It sold more than two million copies in the US alone, and could be said to have comfortably outlasted the forgettable film which it was supposed to augment. How ironic that Jon should choose a mediocre movie through which to take his music to hitherto undreamt of heights. His inspiration is obvious on every track. And, contrary to everybody's expectations, it didn't turn out to be something of a young Springsteen outing. Jon's admiration and adulation of The Boss didn't stretch to emulation. He was content to be his own man - and reaped the rewards accordingly.

'Blaze Of Glory' not only established the fact that, should he wish, Jon could cut mustard as a solo artist in his own right (thereby increasing his stock within the Bon Jovi camp), but also garnered him awards. The title track was voted 'Best Original Song' at the 1990 Golden Globe film awards (one of the most prized ceremonies of the year in the movie world) and gathered up the award for 'Best Pop/Rock Single' at the American Music Awards in January of 1991. It was also nominated for the category of 'Best Original Song In A Film' at the Academy Awards in 1991, being pipped at the post by the legendary Stephen Sondheim and a song he composed for Madonna and the Warren Beatty film 'Dick Tracy'. During the last-named ceremony, Jon performed 'Blaze Of Glory' in company of Richie Sambora, thereby ending speculation at the time that the pair had fallen out very badly.

But if Jon was proud of his achievements as a solo performer - albeit quietly proud of them - he was also working on a much more difficult and long-term project, his own label.

It had long been in Jon's mind to diversify into other areas, but he needed time to get things going. He already had his own production company (perhaps not too surprisingly called New Jersey Inc.). Now, he was setting up a label that he hoped would develop the talents of a number of individuals who had not really been given much of a chance by other companies.

"What I want to do," said Jon at the time, "is to set up something that could be perceived as being independent in spirit. It will be distributed by PolyGram, but won't have the corporate mentality. If you like, I hope you can link it to what Berry Gordy did when he first put Motown together. And because of my own background, I am able to get involved in all aspects of my artists' records. I can write with them, produce them, play on their records. It gives me an advantage that few other record company executives would have. Obviously, I won't be able to compete with the amounts of money a major label can offer a band - this my own personal money weighed against the huge resources of, say, PolyGram - but what I can offer is a more personalised approach. That will appeal to some artists, of that I am sure."

The label was originally to be called Underground Records - a logo was even mocked up similar in style that of the world-famous London Underground logo to be found throughout the UK's capital city. But eventually it was changed to Jambco (standing for Jon, Anthony, Matt Bongiovi Company. Anthony and Matt are of course Jon's two younger brothers). The first signees were the folksy Billy Falcon and, ironically, Aldo Nova.

The Canadian multi-instrumentalist had been a major recording artist for Portrait/Epic back in 1984 when the debut Bon Jovi album had hit. He had lent his talents and reputation to Jon in order to help the young Jersey aspirant. Now, old debts were being paid off.

Jon was actively involved in Aldo's record, 'Blood On The Bricks', and the album clearly benefitted from his involvement. It was one of the best AOR releases of 1991, but sadly failed to set the charts alight, as was also the case with Falcon's unobtrusive release. But that wasn't the point with Jambco; it had been set up to promote music, not necessarily to sell millions. Jon himself kept a tight rein on proceedings and brought his own experiences and expertise to bear.

In recent times, Jambco has pretty much been put on the back burner by Jon, as he again concentrates his efforts and skills in support of Bon Jovi. Aldo Nova has moved on, and at the time of writing only Billy Falcon remains signed to the label - apart, that is, from Bon Jovi themselves.

"Bon Jovi is my priority," Jon told me at the end of 1992. "It is the only thing that interests me right now. I stopped doing outside projects in March '92 after working with Aldo Nova and Billy Falcon on their albums, writing with Hall & Oates and also Stevie Nicks.

"The only thing I've been offered since came from Southside Johnny, who is still one of my heroes. I did 12 shows with him as his rhythm guitarist, touring in a van and playing clubs - it was great. At one point w e sat in the back of the van and talked about his future and what could be done to make him happen again. I told him that I felt he should do various things, such as get Steve Van Zandt and Bruce Springsteen involved. He did everything I suggested and then asked me to come down and help out on his new record. But I was so burnt out and tired that I had to turn it down."

So, what future Jambco? It's not unusual for major bands to form their own labels, in order to provide for themselves greater control over their own product. The Rolling Stones have Rolling Stones Records. Def Leppard have Bludgeon Riffola. But in each of these cases, the only signees to the label are the band who own it. The set-up is not ostensibly there to benefit others. However, Jambco is different in that it hasn't been put into action merely to feather the Bon Jovi nest. This is a serious long-term project that Jon will undoubtedly revive in an active sense when time again permits.

Jambco is yet more proof that Jon is a serious music fan who has an insatiable appetite for the discovery of new bands whenever and wherever he can. He has a constant urge to nurture new talent and to give it breathing room. Jon is one of the very few major stars I have ever had the pleasure of meeting who is an unashamed fan. He would rather be in a sweaty, smokey bar checking out an interesting young band than lording up in a swank club being feted with free drinks from the bar - well, almost anyway! In many respects he shares Prince's philosophy that success has allowed him to pursue his hobby - music! And it should come as no surprise that he is an admirer of the purple Paisley Parketeer.

"I am a big fan of his, and have a lot of time for his attitude. The first time I met him was at a club. He was at a table with various people, surrounded by security guards. Bon Jovi were at another table. Anyway, he invited us to join him and then he came over and joined us. We had great fun and talked about a lot of different things. He was a brilliant guy to be with."

Jon's unshakeable belief in the work ethic is something he shares with Prince. However, unlike the latter, he has always sought to provide succour for the media. It's another way of Jon opening up outlets for his abilities and strengths. Although a drain, Jon Bon Jovi has never shirked his responsibilities as a spokesman for the band. In that he differs from Prince and also Springsteen, who are only answerable to themselves. As he has always been at pains to point out, there are four other members of Bon Jovi to be considered. His foray into solo activity has never altered a deeply felt loyalty to the band who bear his name. In a strange way, whilst the success of 'Blaze Of Glory' clearly strengthened his hand in matters of diplomacy within the band structure, it also made him realise the value of sharing that success.

Whilst Jon was pursuing his activities with an amazing vigour, he wasn't alone in this respect. Richie, in particular, took the opportunity of a break in the Bon Jovi schedule to show what he could do in his own right.

CHAPTER THIRTEEN

RICHIE GETS STRANGE

Richie Sambora has often been undervalued within the Bon Jovi scenario. He was the guitarist. Jon was the founding father. He was the party-loving funster. Jon was the serious musician. There has, of necessity, been a tension between them almost from the beginning. For the most part, this tension was rather positive in establishing the Bon Jovi sound and style. But, being a member of a band must out of necessity mean giving up a certain autonomy of thought and action. Any successful member of a strong unit must be prepared to compromise on certain subjects. This is perhaps true of Richie Sambora rather more than most.

Sambora's talents include not only a remarkable ability to play guitar, but also a creative aspiration when it comes to singing. Richie's vocal sensibility was inevitably stifled somewhat within the Bon Jovi structure. He was able to contribute backing vocals on such magnanimous songs as 'Wanted: Dead Or Alive', but beyond this he had little opportunity to impress with that side of his gifts.

So, when Jon decided that the time was right to put Bon Jovi on ice for a couple of years, Richie took the chance to sign his own solo deal. And thus he set out to put together an album reflecting his own taste and style, under the title of 'Stranger In This Town'.

It was a chance for Richie to show what he could do when let loose - and he took the opportunity in both hands.
"Man, I can't wait for people to hear what I've done," Richie said just after finishing the record. "This isn't a Bon Jovi record at all, but rather one that allows me to take different turns and go all over the place. There's blues in here, R&B. Rock'n'roll. Some shit that Bon Jovi could never do. Of course, there are also points where I do deliver songs that are close to what Bon Jovi are all about...Well, I'm just having so much fun on this record."

Sambora elected to use David Bryan and Tico Torres on this album, as well as bassist Tony Leven (of King Crimson/Anderson, Bruford, Wakeman & Howe fame) and percussionist Gerardo Valez (Spyro Gyra). And Richie also managed to get one of his boyhood heroes onto the album - the great guitarist Eric Clapton.

"The idea of working with Eric came to me when I was asked to present an award to Eric in New York in 1991, at the International Rock Awards," recalls Richie. "It was an honour for me to do that. I also got the chance to play with him, Lou Reed, Buddy Guy and Bo Diddley in a jam session at the same ceremony. It was amazing, no egos or anything.

"Anyway, I wrote the song 'Mr. Bluesman' about a young kid who wants to be a guitarist and is inspired by his hero. It was based to some extent on the way that Eric inspired me. So I got the idea of writing him a letter asking if he'd do me the honour of appearing on the song, explaining the storyline behind it and also how he could relate to it because of the way the likes of Robert Johnson inspired him. I never expected any sort of reply, so imagine my delight when he called me and agreed to do it!."

Richie took full advantage of the celebrated guitarist's acquiescence to fly to London in March 1991 and book time at Air Studios for Clapton to lay down his solo on the song.

"It's the quintessential Clapton solo - he burns," exclaims Richie at the memory. "And he's such a nice guy. We had a long chat after the recording session and I also took the opportunity to present him with a special acoustic guitar that I'd had made for the occasion".

"I remember at one point during the recording process thinking to myself, 'Eric Clapton is here, playing on MY solo album, and I'M producing him!' I just had to stop the tape and ask him why he was doing this for me. He just said that when we were onstage in New York, he felt that I belonged up there with him, Buddy Guy and the others. What a compliment!"

The album was eventually released on the Mercury label, not Jambco as originally intended. The switch came about because Richie withdrew his active support from Jon's label.

"It's true that the label was formed in the first place by Jon and myself, but having thought about it, I just decided that I didn't want to be a record company executive. I just want to concentrate on being an artist. I really just haven't got the mentality for it, I'm afraid."

'Stranger In This Town' wasn't a huge commercial success. In fact, it was something of a flop. But musically, it was nothing short of impressive. Even Jon found time to praise the record.

"I must admit to liking what Richie did. I think he showed a few people that there was more to him than what he does in Bon Jovi. And I have to admit that I would have liked to do 'Stranger In This Town', the title track, on a Bon Jovi album. It would have been great."

Richie summed up the philosophy behind the album thus: "This album is more to my roots and is developed from there. I wanted to take the opportunity to experiment and try out new musical avenues. This is the record I've always wanted to make. You could say that it's been my personal property for 32 years, and now it belongs to everybody. With a band, everyone puts something into the melting pot and what comes out is a conglomeration of all the parts. This record is all about me! Mind you, it was very hard work putting it together, in fact I've never had to work so hard in my life. But it was very fulfilling."

There was a diversity to the album that allowed Richie the chance to explore differing areas of musical texture. The title track, 'Church Of Desire' and 'One Light Burning' were decidedly laid-back, but infectious and possessed of a clamped groove. 'Mr Bluesman' really does provide Sambora and guest Clapton with a vigorous work-out. Indeed, so electrifying is the Clapton solo that one can only feel dreadfully disappointed that the man has not been tempted to follow up this performance with more blues playing on his own albums - such is life and its let-downs. Only on a couple of cuts, in particular 'Rosie' and 'Yesterday's Dreams', does Sambora sail close to Bon Jovi territory. But his own rich tones give even these songs a different stamp to that of Jon's.

With the experienced Neal Dorfsman (Dire Straits) acting as co-producer, Sambora gave us an album that should have provided him with more commercial credence than was to be the case. It took Richie some nine months to complete the project, working on it whenever he had the chance. Dorfsman had commitments to Dire Straits, and Sambora took three weeks out to play in Japan at the end of 1990 with Bon Jovi, climaxing in a special New Year's Eve date that also featured, among others, Skid Row.

Sambora, unlike Jon himself, took the chance to tour his solo album, playing clubs across America. However, plans to take the show to Europe never materialised as sales of the album failed to reach expected levels. But far from being down-hearted, Richie hopes to have the chance to record further solo albums.

"I have a lot more ideas in this vein. They are stockpiled until the opportunity presents itself."

David Bryan was the only other member of Bon Jovi to take full advantage of the opportunity to do a project away from the mother ship. He was asked to compose the instrumental soundtrack for the low-budget horror film 'Netherworld', released through the Full Moon label. Alec John Such unfortunately spent his time, according to Jon, recovering from a bad motorcycle accident.

What lessons each member learnt from going it alone can only be speculated. But as they were to prove in 1992/3, the spirit of togetherness within the band was still very strong. There was an urgent desire from all five members to make things work to their advantage. Jon might have shown that he could go it alone and achieve huge success, Richie might have gained considerable critical acclaim for his own efforts, but what they still needed was each other. They were a combative team who could still bring an extra dimension to the other's talents. However, before they could even consider getting back into a workable professional relationship, there were a few thorns to be excised from the skin. For both men had been critical of one another.

Faith and Glory

CHAPTER FOURTEEN

OH, BUT DID YOU HEAR WHAT HE SAID...

The relationship between any singer and guitarist is always a difficult one. History is full of situations where the one partner has fallen out badly with the other. On most occasions, it is a balance between tension, antipathy and respect that provides for a good partnership. Consider Steven Tyler and Joe Perry (Aerosmith). Mick Jagger and Keith Richards (Rolling Stones). Axl Rose and Slash (Guns n' Roses). Roger Daltrey and Pete Townsend (The Who). All of them have something in common - mutual respect born out of inevitable antagonism. One has only to see the different ways in which the singer and the guitarist in a band are perceived.

The singer is the focal point, the swashbuckling, strutting frontman, the man who inspires sexual fire and ire. He is the obvious pin-up. The guitarist is the musician. He is the real creative force in the line-up - at least as far as the public are concerned. Yet the chemistry of any successful band is such that a good singer to some extent craves respect for his craft, whilst the good guitarist would like some of that attention.

Egos being what they are, it's inevitable that there will be clashes between any singer and guitarist in a hugely popular band. If those clashes can be channelled into positive energy, then you can have a potent and unique force to be reckoned with. It's the bonding of opposites and the fission thereof that makes things happen - and if you don't believe me, just listen to the music thrown up over the years by the aforementioned. And once you have digested the songs, go back and witness the oft-reported public feuding between the pairs. I think you'll agree there is something in what I say.

The relationship between Jon and Richie is no different. It is a remarkable alliance, capable of penning masterpieces, and of delivering them onstage. They are the hub on Bon Jovi. The public face, if you will. I would certainly never denigrate the roles played by Tico, Alec and David in the band, but it is Jon and Richie who have provided the necessary sparkle of genius to take it onto a different plane.

Jon is the workaholic of the pair. He runs the show, because he takes the responsibility for it. He is fully aware and appreciative of the fact that the band bears his name, and so every note and chord of each song is carefully scrutinised in the studio. Each photo session is perused with the expert eye born through experience. Everything that bears the legend 'Bon Jovi' has Jon's seal of approval. He undoubtedly enjoys having a finger in every pie - but sometimes just gives the impression that he wishes Richie in particular would donate the occasional thumbprint.

Richie is a free spirit. He is extremely serious about his music, but reacts to the moment. He co-writes the songs, does his guitar parts and then feels the drive and urge to go and do something else. He hasn't the mechanics and mentality to sit for hour-upon-hour in a studio listening to playbacks of tracks he recorded days ago. He would rather be jamming with blues musicians in a local bar. Therein lies the crucial difference between Jon and Richie.

For the most part, Jon has always accepted this to be the case, but when your energies are drained and you still have reels of tapes to listen to or plans to approve for the next day's interview schedule, or photos to view, or roadies to admonish for messing up a vital part of the stage presentation, and your partner in crime is off sinking a few beers and generally enjoying himself, irritation can creep in. That happened towards the end of the 'New Jersey' tour. Tiredness increased the irritability factor, and by the end of that trek, relations were strained between Jon and Richie. It reached a head when Jon himself reacted to press speculation in the UK that Bon Jovi had, in fact, split up and that the general atmosphere between Jon and Richie was permanently soured. At the time Jon told me:

"Thanks to certain English magazines, claiming that Tico Torres has left the band and some general shit-stirring we are now pretty damn close to splitting up. My attitude now is; if it happens then OK, 'cos I know I'm gonna be around. As for Richie, well there has been a problem between us. Look, I love Richie, but I don't like him this week. It's not his problem, it's mine. I can't cite any reason for a rift between us because there isn't one. But don't tell me to sit at home and watch TV or go to the beach. I can't do it. And if it's Richie, or whoever sitting around, then I'll tell them to get the hell out and leave me alone."

Strong words. But did Jon seriously expect anyone to believe that an article in an English magazine could actually split up Bon Jovi? Well, research leads me to suggest that this is precisely what nearly did happen - or to be more accurate, the news acted as a catalyst. Let me explain. Put yourself in the position of working on a project over a long period in time. It quickly becomes obvious that if things are to get done then it is you who has to take control. You are perfectly prepared to do this, on the understanding that you take a lion's share of the profit. This is agreed with the others on the project. However, as time moves on, you become increasingly irked that, whilst you have this tacit agreement, nonetheless there is never any sign of the others even making the effort to offer you more support. They are content to sit back and take their cut, whilst leaving the bulk of the work on your shoulders. You begin to feel resentment towards the others, although the project is proving a huge success,

Now is the picture becoming clearer? Psychologically, Jon was feeling the drain of almost five years' constant work and pressure. He had taken most of the responsibility for the band on his shoulders, doing the vast majority of the groundwork on all levels in the Bon Jovi cause, on the basis of the fact that he stood to gain most from its success. However, the others were all making considerable sums themselves, yet by the end of the 'New Jersey' tour they were not, in Jon's estimation, giving him all them help they could be. Everything rested on him, and the irritation was building.

At the end of the tour, the frustration being felt by Jon increased another notch when he found that the rest of the band wanted to relax and enjoy their money and fame. They wanted Jon to take a break. Meanwhile, Jon himself wanted to plunge into the next stage of the Bon Jovi game plan. He wanted to take the band to the next level. Finding the others unwilling simply added to his resentment. They were content to leave everything to him - and now to add insult to injury they were telling him they wanted a chance to catch their breath!

That's why, when the offer came to write and perform the soundtrack to 'Young Guns II', Jon took the chance with both hands. That's why when he read that infamous article about Tico being ready to quit the band and problems allegedly between himself and other members of the band, Jon reacted so vehemently. He felt that, after all he had done for the band, if that's the way they wanted to repay him - by quitting- then that was fine by him. There's no smoke without fire, so the magazine report must have some truth to it, right? Jon's response above was meant as a warning shot to the other members of Bon Jovi - if they wished to leave then he wasn't about to stop them. By this time, even though 'Young Guns II' hadn't been issued, Jon knew he was firmly established in his own right. He had sufficient money in the bank never to have to work again, if he so chose. He had a solo career just waiting to happen - and many influential people trying to persuade him to take that option. He had his own label to develop. He had a large number of offers from all quarters to get involved in outside projects. He no longer needed Bon Jovi. He could split the band up tomorrow. But the future of the band rested in what the other four wanted to do - he was committed to the Bon Jovi cause, but were they?

In particular, Jon was striking back at Richie. Of all the members of Bon Jovi, Jon felt most dismayed by Richie's attitude. He was closest to the guitarist in the band. They were a strong writing partnership. But by mid-1990, their differences had become far more important than their bond. And they are two very different people. Nothing could possibly sum up where the difference between the two lay more than in their approach to women.

Jon, despite his good looks and fame, was never especially promiscuous. He had dated Dorothea Hurley for a number of years prior to their marriage. He was keen to settle down into family life. And the birth of his daughter, Stephanie Rosie, in 1993, was one of the proudest moments of his life. Talking in May '93 whilst on tour in Europe, Jon made it plain just how much he loved Dorothea and how greatly he was looking forward to the birth of his first child.

"I am so proud of Dorothea. She has handled the entire pregnancy amazingly well. I just can't believe it. I want to be present at the birth. I have a private jet standing by to take me back home at a moment's notice that things are about to move. And if I can't use the jet, then I'll jump on Concorde or the first available commercial flight!"

Jon also took considerable pride in Dorothea's achievements at the US national karate championships in late 1992, when she came fourth. Domesticity seems to suit Jon to some extent - although it hasn't lowered his work threshold any.

By contrast, Richie has always enjoyed the company of beautiful women. In particular, famous actresses. He had a brief liaison with Ally Sheedy, before in late 1989, beginning an affair with Cher. At this stage in his life, Richie has no intention of following Jon's example and getting married, ready to settle down into a secure future. That's not his style, nor his desire. And Richie carried some of that approach over into his work. He certainly cannot be faulted for his devotion to Bon Jovi, but that would never stretch to spending endless hours in the studio with Jon. He much preferred being at a local bar or club, as I've said before.

But when the guitarist elected to take the opportunity of a break in the Bon Jovi schedule to record a solo album, then he had to take more responsibility for his actions. He was in control, there was simply nobody else he could leave at the mixing desk whilst he spent time on the town. He took to this responsibility with surprising ease, however. And when it came time for Richie to reply to Jon's publicly-stated position, he did so with much thought and diplomacy, whilst also making it clear to Jon that he was still very much committed to Bon Jovi.

"Doing a solo album has shown me that there is life beyond Bon Jovi and I'll continue to do solo albums, because they give me a chance to explore many musical areas. But I am still a member of Bon Jovi and will still continue to be so. I know that Jon is itching to get back into action."

"Jon and I are two very different people and it's inevitable that we should have our disagreements. I'm a happy-go-lucky, essentially fun-loving person, whilst Jon is a workaholic. But, at the end of the day, there is a respect between us. But I doubt whether putting together my solo album has made me more sympathetic towards him. You see I was there every step of the way when all the Bon Jovi albums were being recorded. I saw it all, so doing my own record has given me no fresh insight into what Jon goes through."

"As far as Bon Jovi goes, Jon is right when he says that the problem within Bon Jovi was caused by external forces, such as untrue magazine reports. Bon Jovi has always been a strong unit. Sure, we took an extended break after the 'New Jersey' tour. But we got back together at the end of last year (1990), played a special charity show in New Jersey (every fan had to bring along a tin of food to be distributed to the poor as a BJ festive gift) and then went on to headline a stadium show in Tokyo on New Year's Eve. And our performance that night, in front of 68,000 fans, was one of the best of our career! Does that sound like a band on the verge of splitting up?!"

Richie's relationship with Cher had added fuel to the fire of the problems between Jon and Richie. Whilst Jon had worked with Richie on songs for the chanteuse, nonetheless he has never hidden the fact that he doesn't exactly regard her as one of his closest friends. Richie's ardour has cooled somewhat towards Cher, but it didn't stop the pair spending time together in Madrid during May '93, when Bon Jovi were on the road and Cher was also in town. It was then that Jon made a few things known about the actress/singer.

"We did a very important TV show in America recently, The David Letterman Show. We were gonna play live, but just as we were about to be introduced by David, Cher just walked onstage unannounced and gave him a bottle of the perfume she's promoting! Now David has always had a crush on Cher, so her sudden appearance completely threw him, as you can imagine. It took the spotlight right away from us. But I won't have a lovers' tiff between Cher and Richie affecting this band. She owes me an apology for that performance."

Yet, whatever their differences of opinion and outlook, there has never really been any doubting the mutual respect between Jon and Richie. They are still one of the best songwriting teams in the world, and they do play off each other onstage with a consummate skill and ease. Nothing gave Jon greater pleasure than to know that he still had Richie's full backing and support. As October 1991 dawned, Jon began the process of seeing whether Bon Jovi did indeed have any sort of future. The five members got together for the first time in several months. It was time for the moment of truth to dawn...

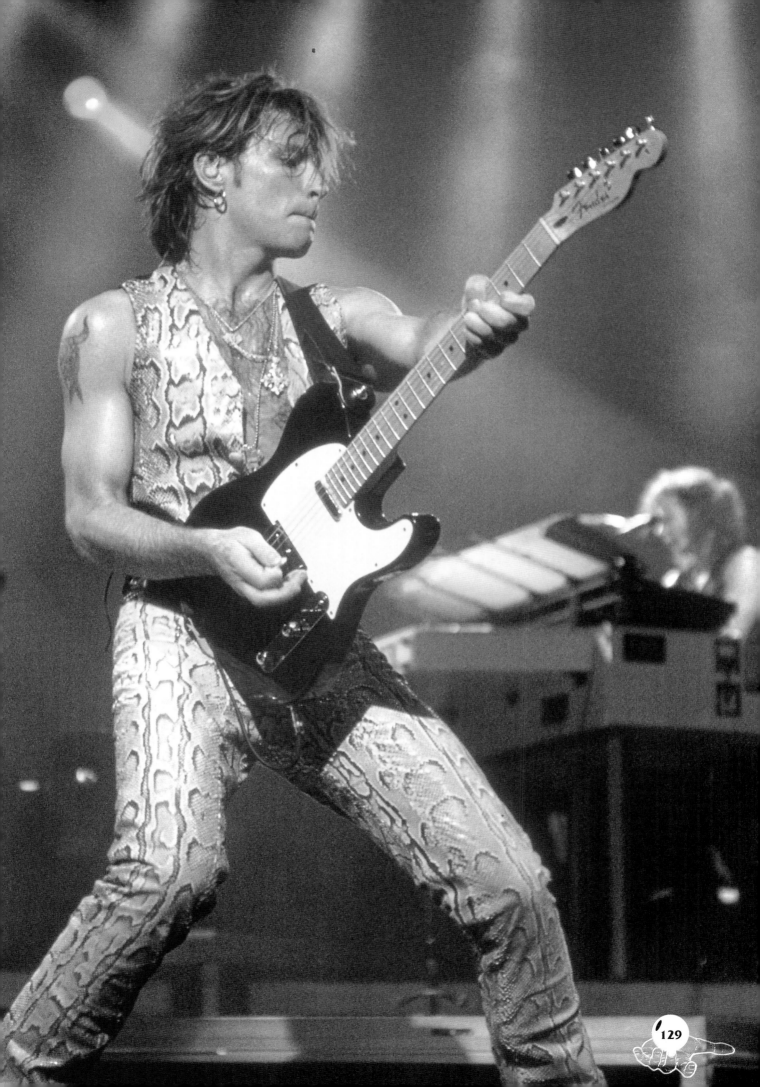

BON JOVI

Keep The Faith

CHAPTER FIFTEEN

REDISCOVERING THE FAITH

Could Bon Jovi work together again? After all the accusations and counter-accusations, was there any chance of the five hauling themselves out of the mire and rediscovering their touch? More to the point, did they want to do so? That's what Jon had to find out. He had plans in place for Bon Jovi, but needed the full support of the others to make them work.

"We had a meeting," recalls Jon. "I said, 'We are going away for a week to talk over plans for the future'. I told my family that if I was home before Saturday then it wasn't good. We went to an island in the Caribbean called St.Thomas. We all stayed together in one house - no wives, no girlfriends, no managers, no agents. Just the five of us. There was only one road leading to the airport, so if anyone left they could be seen! I had a bunch of songs written and we discussed ideas and hung out together. I wanted to see if we were all thinking on the same wavelength."

The problems of the previous year or so, the magazine reports, Jon's own feelings at the end of the 'New Jersey' tour and also the solo commitments of various people within the band - all of these finally came to a head on St. Thomas. It was time for Jon to find out whether he wanted to move forward with these musicians - or to move on. If the outcome of this get together had been inimical rather than amicable, and if Jon had come home feeling anything other than total support from Richie, David, Tico and Alec, then I believe Bon Jovi would have been buried there and then.

Jon had shown he no longer needed Bon Jovi for commercial success. He could strike out on his own. But he didn't want the band to merely disintegrate and fizzle into history. He did his utmost to accommodate the others. But he also needed to know they wanted to carry on, not because of Bon Jovi's money-making potential, but because they still had pride in their music and in this band. He came back home satisfied.

Faith and Glory

Only five people know exactly what was said during that week. Only five people know how close Bon Jovi came to splitting up back then. But whatever the truth of the situation, there was a renewed bonding between the quintet. They were, once again, blood brothers of the road. Jon, presumably, didn't expect the others to have radically changed, but he must have hoped that Richie's solo excursions had made him more sympathetic (despite the guitarist's protestations to the contrary) towards his own work ethic and to what it takes in terms of spending hour-upon-dreary-hour poring over spools of tapes in order to make the best possible album. And David's brief foray into the world of solo recording for the 'Netherworld' soundtrack must also have provided him with more of an insight into having the buck stop with you!

Jon also had to search through his own heart and to ask himself? Do I still want to carry on with Bon Jovi? The answer came back loud and clear: OF COURSE I DO. One reason for this was his admiration of each and every member of his band. Witness what he told Metal CD magazine: "The guys in the band don't get their just rewards. I'll bet my nuts Tico could take any one of the guys in any one of these popular bands and kick their dicks in the dirt. He's so diverse. But he doesn't get his reward because the style of music that he's asked to play behind the songs I write has to be a certain way.

"Richie's never going to be Eddie Van Halen. But he never wanted to be Eddie Van Halen. His heart was in being like Johnny Winter and Eric Clapton. He wanted to develop his style as a blues-based player - and I admire him for that. David, with his toes, can play better than those who beat him in the polls for 'Best Keyboard Player'. He's been playing classical music for more than 20 years. But you can't demand respect, you can't beg for respect, all you can do is survive. And that's probably the greatest testament to our work - to be around ten years, be around 15 years, come back in 20 and take a bow."

But once the green light for the continuation of Bon Jovi had been given, there was much preparation that needed to be done in order to make the 'comeback' album a success. Not least in the fact that the band chose to part company with long-time manager Doc McGhee. The reasons for this split were purely business-associated. There was no falling out on a personal level between Jon and Doc. It was simply a case that Doc had diversified his interests, not only managing an increasing roster of bands (the Scorpions had been recent additions to his list of clients), but also getting into non-music related businesses. Jon felt that, given this situation, Doc could no longer provide him with the priority attention that had been his lot for the previous few years - attention that the singer now felt Bon Jovi required more than ever if their return to duty was to be the success it needed to be.

Keep The Faith

"Doc was there from the beginning and he was also a friend," says Jon. "But his interests have diversified; eventually the fact that he has got into other businesses whilst my seven days a week, 24 hours a day attitude hasn't changed finally caught up with him. Apart from a brief meeting I haven't seen Doc in more than a year, but if he were here right now, I'd certainly have a cup of coffee with him and shoot the shit."

Replacing Doc proved a very difficult task for Jon.

"After leaving Doc, I made a short list of six managers whom I wanted to talk to about looking after the band. In the end, though, I spoke to 26 managers. In fact, I got to the stage when I would talk to anyone who had something to offer. But I couldn't find the right person to suit us."

The difficulty facing Jon was inevitable. He had been used to getting Doc's full attention. Moreover, Doc understood Jon and his ways of working. To get the right person to step into McGhee's shoes was a Herculean task. It required somebody of stature, who was prepared to spend their time dealing with Bon Jovi. It needed someone who could also help take the band to the next level. But Jon couldn't find anyone who fitted the bill, so he elected to take on the management of the band himself - or, to be more specific, he formed BJM, Bon Jovi Management, a self management set-up. He staffed the company with people like Paul Korzilius and Margaret Sterlacci whom he had worked with for some years, and felt had the competence and trustworthiness to make the operation a success. He was guaranteed a managerial set-up cast to suit his aspirations, one that would also have the clout to make things happen.

"The company only looks after Bon Jovi, that's what it's there for. And if any member of the band wants help on outside projects, then of course all the facilities would be at his disposal."

138

Once this side of the business had been sorted out, Jon and the rest of the band threw themselves with utter conviction and commitment into making the best album they could. In January 1993, Bon Jovi began the lengthy process of assembling the material for the record, having to briefly postpone plans in order to allow Richie to finish his touring commitments in support of 'Stranger In This Town'. In the end they spent six months at Little Mountain Studios with Bob Rock occupying the production seat. "We had never spent six months before doing an album. But it's the way Bob Rock has become in the last few years. He's a superhuman producer."

Ultimately, the album, 'Keep The Faith', turned out to be the best Bon Jovi release thus far. It had a maturity of approach and style that certainly took the band to a new level of musical achievement. The album had a certain class. It sounded relaxed yet not lazy, tight yet not stifling. And the songs were filled with momentous musical vignettes and some supreme JBJ lyricism. If there could ever have been any doubt about Bon Jovi's longevity, then 'Keep The Faith' surely dampened them. With one bound, the five-piece had left behind them the pop-rock tag of yore and acquired a new respect as a truly great rock band who could transcend genres and categorisation.

The album opener, 'I Believe', sets the tone with a bracing surge of controlled rhythms and tutored guitars, as Jon wails an impassioned set of lyrics. The title track is the affirmation of the band's renewed commitment to each other, as evinced with the sleeve photo of five hands bonding together. It is also a strong message to the world never to give up hope - one of Jon's true beliefs. Every song on this record is set fair in a powerfully splayed arrangement. Each is lovingly crafted and styled. And they are also tracks very close to Jon's heart.

"I wrote most of the material on the album myself. A lot of what's going on lyrically this time is in the first person narrative. It's not me hiding behind fictional characters, as has been the case in the past. I'm disclosing more about me than ever before."

Nothing sums this up better than 'Bed Of Roses', written by Jon when he was alone in a hotel room wondering about whether Bon Jovi had any sort of future. Jon was in an uneasy frame of mind and it is reflected beautifully in the song. Few lyricists of the modern era could better bring deep emotion to the surface, capture it and then present it for others in a way that was so readily accessible. A true artist at work. 'Dry County' is similarly evocative, painting a sweeping canvas with words.

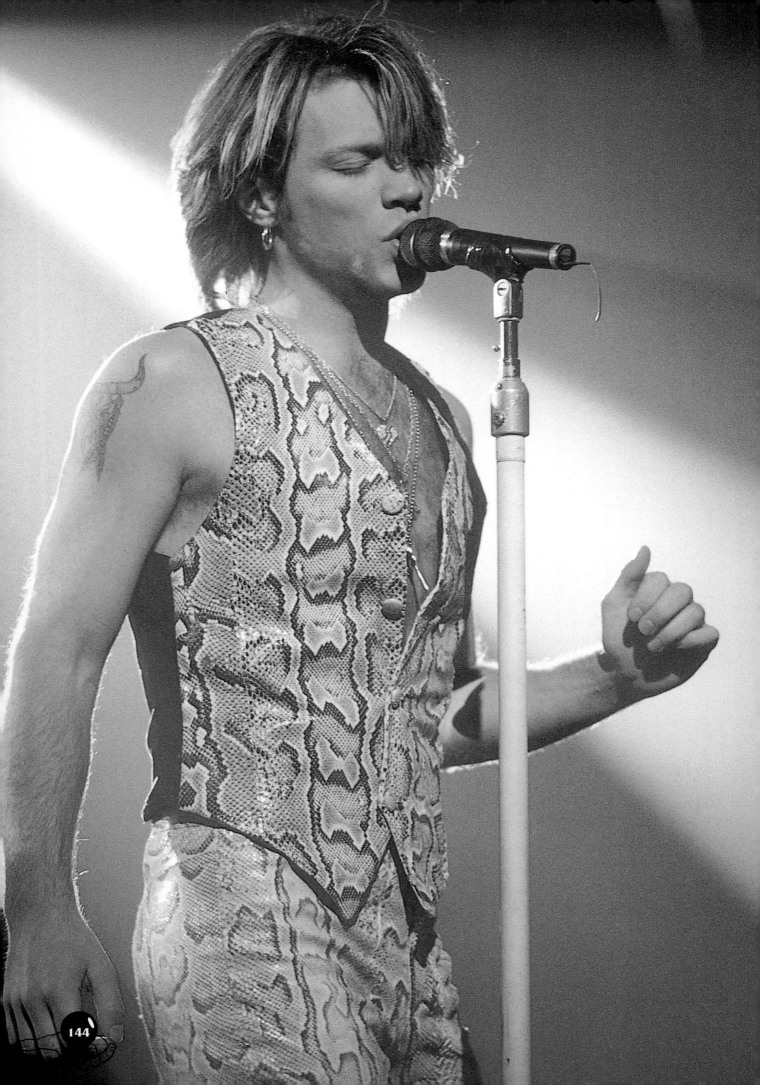

Of course, there were the more uptempo and glorious vanities, such as 'In These Arms', with its instant Bon Jovi insignia. And 'Blame It On The Love Of Rock & Roll' brings to the fore the attitude of those who simply cannot get enough of spirit that has always driven zestful music. It's a powerhouse furnace of classic anthemic proportions, as Jon kicks in with biting words about standing up for wearing your hair long and wrapping your soul in denim'n'leather and brushwood characterisation. 'I'll Sleep When I'm Dead' is a glad-rag roar that underpins Jon's philosophy of never wasting a waking moment.

"This is a Bon Jovi record for the '90s," proclaims Jon. "You know, I can never repeat old formulae. There is no point in going backwards, that's just bullshit. And we also cannot just follow the current trend, because there's no satisfaction in that either. Look, when we started out, Boy George was a major star. But where is he now? Since then, many fashions have come and gone. If we'd have latched onto every single trend that's happened we'd be a musical mess by now!"

"We have to believe in what we do. There's no point in doing a Garth Bon Jovi record or moving to Seattle. What's the use? All I know is that I'm happy with the record we've put out, and that's matters most to me because I made this record for myself."

One unusual approach taken this time around by Jon was to experiment with the notion of remixes. A number of acts these days bring in technocrats to strip down songs and rebuild them in the image of a different medusa - it's almost like presenting a new song to the world. The trouble is that the artist loses control of his original vision, and relies totally on someone else's talents. Bon Jovi brought in Mike Edwards, mainman of British electro-rockers Jesus Jones, to remix 'Keep The Faith' (the song, not the album). But the results didn't meet with Jon's total approval and has remained under wraps.

"He did an acid-house remix and it was a great job. But on hearing it, I just thought that I hadn't actually been involved in the process. It was somebody else's work. And how on earth could I do it onstage? In the end I felt that it didn't really fit in with this band's approach. We are a rock band, not an acid-house outfit. Here we were in danger of getting into foreign territory. And how would Bon Jovi fans react to it?"

Nobody has a stronger handle on what Bon Jovi could and should be than Jon himself. He is aware that there are boundaries across which Bon Jovi should not traverse, even if the temptation is there. BJ can sound contemporary without resorting to emulating others and using state-of-the-art production trickery.

BONJOVI

Keep The Faith

But, the reaction to 'Keep The Faith' from the critics was mixed. Many failed to appreciate that the band they had recalled from the late '80s had grown up and changed-matured. There was new dimension to the vigour of Bon Jovi. The time away from each other had allowed each of them to develop their skills and open up fresh horizons. 'Keep The Faith' showed them to have come back together with a sense of appreciation of each other. They also brought heightened skills into the band. It worked magnificently, but of course to some Bon Jovi couldn't win for losing - change and you are accused of changing, thereby losing much of what made you attractive in the first place. Refuse to change, and you are accused of standing still, of repeating a formula.

But if the critics failed, in some respects, to see Bon Jovi for what they had become, then the fans were certainly not guilty of such a glaring mistake. They bought the album in droves, taking sales beyond seven million copies, which in times of hardship, recession and stress was quite remarkable. Bon Jovi achieved an artificial level of sales with 'Slippery When Wet' that few have ever attained. It made them the biggest selling act of 1987. But such sales figures are not possible to sustain, because they rely not just on a true fan base, but also on casual sales picked up through those who buy records on the basis of trends and fashions. A select number of acts have gained such figures over the years, each in turn has dropped back to a plateau of regular sales that is more representative of their stature. Bon Jovi are no different. Their current level of around seven million units worldwide puts them up in the highest echelons.

Inevitably, the band hit the road for an extensive tour which showed that their strength as a live band was unimpaired by their absence. Astutely adjusting the ticket prices in the America to reflect the dire economic conditions that still prevailed and had ruined many tours over the past couple of years, the band proved they were as sharp and tight as ever - if not more so. And Europe was crazier over the band than ever. In Madrid, for instance, the band received a police motorcycle escort to and from the gig. Or at least four members of the band did, Jon having gone down early to the gig in his usual manner to oversee operations and ensure everything was running smoothly.

"I bet Richie is happy to be back in a position where he doesn't have to worry about being in the studio or at the gig every single moment, overseeing things," laughs Jon about the current state of his relationship with the guitarist. "Again, he can go out and jam with blues musicians in the local club."

Jon took out a voice teacher on the road, determined to ensure that his vocal chords were kept in the finest trim. He has also learnt a lot about pacing.

"Bruce Springsteen told me that when he was my age he never did as many shows in a row as we've been doing. It is very wearing on the throat, and maybe I've been overdoing it a bit. So I'm cutting back on the number of dates we do straight off."

There is little doubt that the situation in terms of workload within the band hasn't really changed much since they regrouped. Jon is very much at the helm and the focal point of all activity. But the back-up is now more positive from Richie, David, Tico and Alec - the difficulties they encountered on a personal level seems to have had a purging and cleansing effect.

The band's support band in Europe was none other than Rockhead, Bob Rock's band - again an example of Jon wanting to give a friend a break, although it must be stressed that Rockhead would never have got the slot if Jon wasn't convinced they were a band worthy of his backing. And, in typical fashion, Bon Jovi found time on a pre-release promotional trip to play a charity show at London's Astoria Theatre, again taking the opportunity to play their own favourite cover versions. The sight of Jon that night stage-diving into the audience was one to treasure! The proceeds from the gig were of course donated once more to the Nordoff-Robbins Foundation. In November 1990, the band had been honoured for previous work they'd done on behalf of the charity by being given the special Silver Clef Award at a special lunch in New York.

"We only agreed to undertake the promotional trip in the first place if we could do a gig like this at The Astoria. And we enjoyed the experience so much, just getting up there onstage and having fun. We carried on that idea when we started out on the road, just doing the occasional club show. Getting out there is what matters. You know, I would gladly do all this for free as long as I could carry on making records and playing onstage."

And one of the great triumphs of the entire tour came on September 18/19, when the Jovis returned to the Milton Keynes Bowl to play two sold-dates, on a bill also including Billy Idol, The Manic Street Preachers and Little Angels. Jon had considered the likes of Vince Neil and Poison for the bill, but eventually settled on the above trio.

Keep The Faith

BON JOVI

After the first show on September 18 had been announced, Jon was considering the possibility of doing a free show at Hyde Park, but settled for a second date at the Bowl (revamped and going under the name of the National Bowl).

The question now has to be faced as to where Bon Jovi go from here. All of Jon's dreams have been fulfilled, so what is there left for him and the band?

CHAPTER SIXTEEN

INTO THE FUTURE

It's always difficult to predict the future. Back in 1985 I would certainly have never predicted that Bon Jovi would have achieved so much in so many different ways. So, as I sit down and ask the question of 'what now?', I must confess to being just a tad nervous. Don't blame me, if this is all wrong, OK?

Bon Jovi as a band would seem to be stronger than ever - the fires of antagonism having drawn them closer together - and it would seem unlikely that Jon himself would choose this particular time to put Bon Jovi back on ice. But don't be surprised if the next instalment of the Bon Jovi campaign takes in a compilation album of sorts - either live or studio, or a combination thereof. True, 'Keep The Faith' was re-issued in the UK to coincide with the Milton Keynes dates with a free eight-track live CD, but a more extensive work would seem to be a definite future project.

"We have lots of live tapes from various tours at our disposal. It's just a case of going through them," explains Jon.

Any Bon Jovi live album or studio compilation would not be a mere rehash or cash-in, that's not Jon's way. He would demand the highest standards and certainly would expect the final product to be a worthy addition to the Jovi catalogue. And there again, maybe Bon Jovi will cut the grass from under my feet and go straight back into the studio during 1994 and record another studio album before even considering such items as live albums and compilations. There is a renewed vigour and spirit within the band that could well inspire them to explore this avenue without fuss or fanfare.

Jon is almost certain to want to pursue a solo album at some point in the future, perhaps sooner than many people might expect. Although 'Keep The Faith' was the closest yet to a true Jon Bon Jovi solo album - the others, whilst not reduced to mere backing musicians, did have less to do with the album than any previous BJ LP - nonetheless any record put together by Jon outside of Bon Jovi (and also not having the restriction of being a soundtrack record) might well take on a more diverse aspect; it might even employ a style that reflects Jon's respect the R&B style of Bruce Springsteen and Southside Johnny.

BON JOVI

Richie has also stated that he will record more solo albums. The lack of success for 'Stranger In This Town' won't deter him from enjoying the full range of his considerable musical talents. And David is also likely to want the chance to explore other musical avenues - including new age music, in which he has an interest.

Whether we shall see solo projects from either Alec or Tico would not seem to be a point of discussion - the chances are remote. However, both are talented enough to guest with any number of musicians or bands.

Jon has also left the considerable option open of expanding the Jambco label, and signing new acts. He might also explore production with other bands. But Jon the family man will also come to the fore. He is intensely proud of his wife and new daughter. Prior to her birth, Jon spoke about taking the baby on the road with him. He also joked about calling the baby 'Elvis' whatever the sex turned out to be! Unfortunately, there were those who took him seriously when he made this statement. But then that's their problem, right? Talk of any expansion plans in Jon's family, however, are both premature and no-one's business but Dorothea and Jon's.

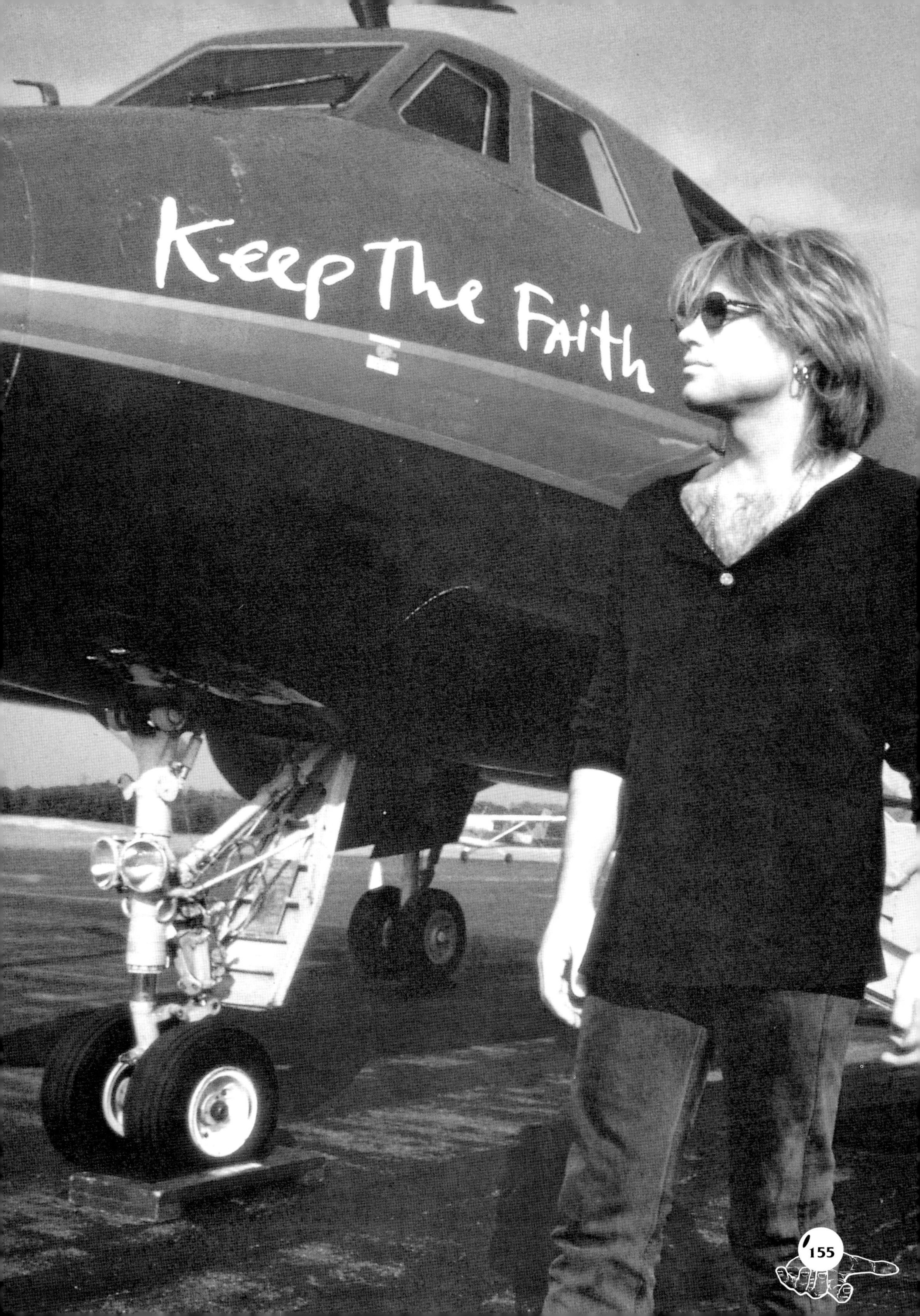
Keep The Faith

JOVI

In May last year, Bon Jovi celebrated sales of 40 million albums worldwide in their ten years together ("The guys asked me what I was gonna give them to commemorate our tenth anniversary!" laughs Jon at the memory), a phenomenal achievement that was marked with a spectacular party hosted by PolyGram Records at famed producer George Martin's newly opened Air Studios in north west London, which is a lavishly converted church. The place was a gothic haven, with wine and beer on tap and giant split screens showing the classic horror movie 'Lust For A Vampire'. It was an impressive way to underpin Bon Jovi's continuing stature as one of the world's greatest rock bands. Definitely one of the social highlights of '93 for those who move in exalted rock circles.

But let's leave the last word to Jon himself, the architect of this genuine rags-to-riches story: "When we were in Little Mountain Studios recording 'Keep The Faith' we had a giant screen erected and it was constantly playing Rolling Stones movies. That's a band who have influenced me greatly in spirit. They've written some great songs, survived anything and everything that could be thrown at them. I went to see them on their last tour in 1989 with a real chip on my shoulder, I have to confess. You see I'd seen them in 1981 and they were great. But eight years later, well, I could sell out the stadium they were playing in, no problem. And that had me feeling perhaps a little blasé about the whole set-up. But I came away in a state of awe, rather like a little kid. They were just amazing. I don't believe Bon Jovi can ever be what they are. Just to carry their luggage would be a privilege.

Faith and Glory

"The sad thing about today is that there's no myth left in music, a lot of the magic's gone. There is so much media coverage of every little thing that nothing is left to the imagination. The excitement has gone out of rock'n'roll in that respect. I remember just lying on my bed with the Stones' 'Sticky Fingers' and Bruce Springsteen's 'Born To Run' albums, just looking at the covers. That was all part of the cool associated with the Stones and Bruce. That doesn't happen any more. I feel it's sad. It would be hard to produce stars of that magnitude anymore. It's gone forever".

"There's an old joke that if you can't sing, you can't write songs and you can't play a musical instrument then somebody can make you a star. But now you don't even have to look any good. There are camera lenses that can do anything you want them to. Make you look thin when you're fat, tall when you're short - anything is possible. As for music, I certainly don't listen to what is trendy. I still listen to classic rock music."

Jon Bon Jovi might be correct in his assessment that in general the times mitigate against the emergence of true stars, but he himself is an exception to this rule. Jon conducts himself like a true star - there is something special about him, but he doesn't flaunt it and he certainly doesn't believe it gives him the right to act in a selfish or unacceptable fashion. Most of all, though, Jon is a survivor. Bon Jovi aren't reliant on the swish of trends or the vagaries of fashion. They have carved out a niche for themselves that will not be worn away by the passage of time. Their achievements are a matter of record. And, who knows, the best might yet lie ahead.

Faith and Glory